THE OFFICIAL BRIDGE BOOK SERIES

IMPROVING YOUR JUDGMENT 1

Opening the Bidding

Audrey Grant

Published by
Baron Barclay Bridge Supplies

Improving Your Judgment 1: Opening the Bidding
Copyright © 2006 Audrey Grant's Better Bridge Inc.

To contact the author, see page 165.

Baron Barclay
3600 Chamberlain Lane, Suite 206
Louisville, KY 40241
U.S. and Canada: 1-800-274-2221
Worldwide: 502-426-0410
FAX: 502-426-2044
www.baronbarclay.com

ISBN 0-939460-37-8

Illustrations by Kelvin Smith
Design and composition by John Reinhardt Book Design

Printed in the United States of America

Contents

Introduction		vii
Audrey's Coded Cards		viii
Acknowledgments		ix
1	*Opening at the One Level—In First and Second Position*	1
	Opening 1NT	2
	Responding to an Opening Bid of 1NT	4
	Opening One-of-a-Suit	8
	The Guideline (Rule) of 20	10
	Responding to an Opening Bid of One-of-a-Suit	12
	Improving Your Judgment	14
	Summary	19
	Quiz	20
	Sample Deals	24
2	*Opening at the One Level—In Third and Fourth Position*	33
	Borderline Openings in Third Position	34
	Borderline Openings in Fourth Position	36
	The Effect of Vulnerability	39
	Responding to Opening Bids in Third and Fourth Position	40
	Improving Your Judgment	43

Contents

Summary		47
Quiz		48
Sample Deals		52

3 Obstructive Opening Bids — 61

Playing Tricks	61
The Guideline (Rule) of 500	63
Openings at the Three Level or Higher	65
Responding to Three-Level or Higher Preemptive Opening Bids	68
The Weak Two-Bid	72
Responding to a Weak Two-Bid	74
Improving Your Judgment	76
Summary	81
Quiz	82
Sample Deals	86

4 Strong Opening Bids — 95

Responding to a Strong Artificial 2♣ Opening	96
Handling Strong Balanced Hands	101
Handling Strong Unbalanced Hands	104
Improving Your Judgment	106
Summary	109
Quiz	110
Sample Deals	114

Practice Deals

Deal #1	24
Deal #2	26
Deal #3	28
Deal #4	30
Deal #5	52
Deal #6	54
Deal #7	56
Deal #8	58
Deal #9	86
Deal #10	88

Contents

Deal #11   90
Deal #12   92
Deal #13   114
Deal #14   116
Deal #15   118
Deal #16   120

Additional Practice Deals   123
Deal #17   124
Deal #18   126
Deal #19   128
Deal #20   130
Deal #21   132
Deal #22   134
Deal #23   136
Deal #24   138
Deal #25   140
Deal #26   142
Deal #27   144
Deal #28   146
Deal #29   148
Deal #30   150
Deal #31   152
Deal #32   154

Glossary   157

The Bridge Basics Series

1 An Introduction
2 Competitive Bidding
3 Popular Conventions
4 Declarer Play
5 Defense

The Improving Your Judgment Series

1 Opening the Bidding
2 Doubles

...more to come

Introduction

If you're reading this book, you're likely an active person interested in ways to improve your bridge game. A closer look at the first bid and the impact it has on the entire auction can dramatically improve your results.

The best theorists in the world have shared their secrets with me, and I am committed to bringing this bridge wisdom to you in a manner which I hope you'll find readable. The material in this book can improve your opening bids... but the concepts will spread and help to improve your judgment in all aspects of the game.

Bidding conversations are effective when they are simple, yet accurate. Both partners have to be comfortable during the auction. The goal is to experience the excitement of the bidding conversation without the stress. I've often said that I don't want a point or two to come between friends. I hope you'll feel the same way after reading this book. To help practice all the concepts, there are four deals at the end of each chapter and sixteen additional deals at the end. Each deal has useful hints on bidding, play, and defense with the key points highlighted. To make it easy to deal out the hands, there are Coded Cards available (see next page).

Congratulations for being interested in an activity that is a wonderful life skill, a game to develop and maintain mental fitness, and a way to spend time with friends whether they're in your neighborhood or from another part of the world.

All the best,

Audrey Grant
www.AudreyGrant.com

Audrey's Coded Cards

For each book in the Improving Your Judgment series there is a companion deck of color-coded cards available (see page 166) which is designed to make it easy to deal and play all thirty-two practice deals.

To use the cards, place the guide card that accompanies the deck in the center of the table.

Distribute each of the cards according to the color-coding on the back. To distribute Deal #7, for example, look at the box numbered 7 on the back of each card. If the box is red, the card goes to North; if it is blue, the card goes to East; yellow goes to South; green goes to West.

Check that each player has thirteen cards. The dealer is indicated by an underline of the number in the box. It is also indicated on the guide card. The deal is then ready to be bid and played...and replayed as often as desired.

If you are practicing by yourself, turn all four hands face up on the table, dummy style (see page 7) and walk through the bidding and play, using the text as a guide where necessary.

If you don't have the color-coded cards, sort a deck of cards into suits and construct the four hands one suit at a time.

Have Fun!

Acknowledgments

To my husband, *David Lindop*, a world-class player who works hand-in-hand with me to produce the bridge books.

To *Jason Grant-Lindop* and *Joanna Grant* for their support and involvement in the many aspects of Better Bridge.

To the Better Bridge Advisory Committee:

- *Bob Hamman* — World Champion, top-ranked male player
- *Petra Hamman* — World Champion, bridge teacher
- *Shawn Quinn* — World Champion, top-ranked female player
- *Fred Gitelman* — Founder of Bridge Base Inc., gold medalist
- *Henry Francis* — Member of the Bridge Hall of Fame, Editor of the Official Encyclopedia of Bridge
- *Jerry Helms* — Professional bridge teacher and player

To Robert Williams, Associate Dean Emeritus, N.C. State University, for his help in editing the book.

To the bridge teachers. Your dedication, skill, and professionalism have made me proud to be counted among you.

To the students of the game-thank you for sharing your ideas and your enthusiasm.

Don't leave home without the
Rule of 20.

—MARTY BERGEN, TO OPEN OR NOT TO OPEN, 2003

Opening at the One Level— In First and Second Position

The serve in tennis, the opening in a chess game, and the first *bid* in an auction all create the drama associated with making the first move. There are a number of guidelines to help make a good decision when you're given the chance to open the bidding. The focus of this book is to provide tips for improving your judgment when you are in this important position.

The first step is to estimate the worth of your hand. There are two features to take into consideration: the *strength* and the *distribution*. When assessing strength, there is general agreement about the value of *high cards*. An ace is worth 4 points, a king 3 points, a queen 2 points, and a jack 1 point.

To assess the value of distribution, most experts suggest counting length as a good measure of the worth of a hand until a trump fit has been found. Add one point for each card beyond four in a suit. A five-card suit is worth 1 point, a six-card suit 2 points, and so on.

Unbalanced hands are usually evaluated by their *trick-taking potential* instead of their point count. If you held all thirteen spades, for example, the value would be far more than 10 *high-card points* plus 9 *length points* since you could take all the tricks if spades were trump.

This chapter will focus on opening the bidding in *first* or *second position*[1]—when you are the dealer or the opponent on your right deals and passes. You'll see how to use the *Rule of 20*, more accurately described as the *Guideline of 20*, and other principles to evaluate borderline hands when you have to decide whether to open the bidding at the one level or pass.

Think of opener as the *describer* and responder as the *decider*, the decision maker. Your objective as opener is to give as clear a picture of your hand as you can in one bid.

Opening 1NT

An opening bid of 1NT paints the most specific picture of the strength and distribution of a hand.

Strength

The strength required for a 1NT opening bid is limited to a narrow three-point range. The most popular range is 15–17 points. We're going to work with that range in this book. There's nothing wrong with other ranges and, once you are familiar with the general concepts, you can develop a bidding style that suits your partnership.

With 5-3-3-2 distribution, add 1 length point for the five-card suit. As a result, 1NT can be opened with only 14 high-card points[2].

Distribution

A notrump opening bid shows a *balanced hand*, a hand with no *voids*, no *singletons*, and no more than one *doubleton*. Three hand patterns fit this description:

---

[1] Sometimes referred to as first or second chair or first or second seat.

[2] If this is your partnership style, the range is typically indicated as 14+–17 rather than 15–17.

x x x x	x x x x	x x x x x
x x x	x x x x	x x x
x x x	x x x	x x x
x x x	x x	x x
4-3-3-3	4-4-3-2	5-3-3-2

You don't need high cards in every suit. The modern style is to open 1NT even when you have a doubleton with two low cards[3]. When opening 1NT with 5-3-3-2 distribution, the five-card suit can be a major[4].

EXAMPLES

You are the dealer, in first position. What *call* would you make with each of the following hands?

♠ A K 3
♥ K J 7
♦ K 9 8 5
♣ J 8 5

1NT. With 15 high-card points and balanced distribution, this hand is ideal for a 1NT opening bid if the partnership has agreed to a range of 15-17 points[5].

♠ Q 10 7 4
♥ A Q 3
♦ A Q
♣ Q 7 6 2

1NT. There are 16 high-card points and the distribution is balanced with only one doubleton.

♠ K 10
♥ K J 4
♦ Q J 8 6 3
♣ A Q 9

1NT. This hand is worth 17 points, 16 high-card points plus 1 length point for the five-card diamond suit. The distribution is balanced since there is only one doubleton.

---

[3] Some players avoid opening 1NT when all the high cards are concentrated in two suits.

[4] Some players still prefer to open one of the major suit.

[5] If your partnership uses another range, such as 12-14 or 16-18, you would open 1♦.

♠ K Q 9 5
♥ 8 4
♦ K J 10 8
♣ A Q J

1NT. There are 16 high-card points and the distribution is balanced. Today's players no longer worry about holding a worthless doubleton for a 1NT opening bid and a 2NT opening bid. 1NT doesn't end the auction; it merely sends a descriptive message to partner.

♠ K 10
♥ Q J 8 6 3
♦ K J 4
♣ A Q 9

1NT. Open 1NT even holding a five-card major. If you open 1♥ and partner responds 1♠, for example, you have a difficult task finding a *rebid* that shows the strength of the hand[6].

♠ Q J 8
♥ A 10 5
♦ K 9
♣ K J 10 9 5

1NT. There are only 14 high-card points but you can add 1 length point for the five-card club suit to bring the total to 15. Although some players would open 1♣, most experts prefer the more aggressive choice of 1NT. The partnership tends to bid more accurately after a 1NT opening than after an opening bid of one of a suit.

Responding to an Opening Bid of 1NT

A big advantage of the 1NT opening bid is that it narrowly defines opener's strength and distribution. That usually allows responder to decide How High and Where the partnership belongs with little or no additional information.

How High

Opener has shown at least 15 and at most 17 points. Responder adds the points shown by opener to those in responder's hand. Responder can usually decide How High immediately. For example:

---

[6] Some players still prefer to open the major suit.

OPENER	RESPONDER	TOTAL	HOW HIGH
15-17	0-7	24 or fewer	Partscore
15-17	10-15	25 or more	Game[7]
15-17	18+	33 or more	Slam

Sometimes responder needs more information from opener:

OPENER	RESPONDER	TOTAL	HOW HIGH
15-17	8-9	23-26	Maybe Game
15-17	16-17	31-34	Maybe Slam

In these situations, responder can make a bid that invites opener to bid game or slam with the top of the range for the 1NT opening. For example, with about 8 or 9 points responder can make an *invitational* raise to 2NT; with 16 or 17 points responder can invite to a small slam by raising to 4NT.

Where

When the partnership is headed for game, responder looks for an eight-card or longer major suit. If there is no major suit fit, responder usually chooses 3NT because game in a minor suit, 5♣ or 5♦, requires two more tricks than game in notrump. If the partnership is stopping in partscore, any eight-card or longer fit can be considered for a trump suit[8].

With a six-card or longer suit, responder knows there is at least an eight-card fit, since opener has at least a doubleton. When responder has a five-card suit, there will be an eight-card or longer fit if opener has three or more cards in the suit. The partnership methods will usually allow responder to investigate whether there is a fit. For

---

[7] Some authorities recommend 26 or more points, but the modern trend is to be more aggressive. The rewards for making a game contract outweigh the occasional penalties for getting too high.

[8] The scoring is more rewarding for notrump and major suit contracts, so this can have an impact on responder's decision, especially in duplicate bridge.

example, when holding a four-card major suit, responder can use the *Stayman convention* with an invitational or stronger hand to find out whether opener has four cards in the major. A response of 2♣ asks opener to bid 2♥ with four or more hearts, 2♠ with four or more spades, or 2♦ with no four-card or longer major.

Another popular convention when responding to 1NT is *Jacoby transfer bids*. A response of 2♦ asks opener to bid 2♥ and a response of 2♥ asks opener to bid 2♠. One advantage of transfer bids is that opener, who usually holds the stronger hand, will become declarer when the partnership plays in a major suit.

Combining How High and Where

If the partnership does not use Jacoby transfer bids, responder can use the following guidelines when responding to 1NT:

Responding to 1NT

- With 0-7 points: Bid 2♦, 2♥, or 2♠ with a five-card or longer suit. These are signoff bids.
- With 8-9 points: With a four-card or longer major suit, use the Stayman convention. With no four-card or longer major suit, bid 2NT. This is an invitational bid.
- With 10-15 points: Bid 4♥ or 4♠ with a six-card or longer major suit. These are signoff bids. Bid 3♥ or 3♠ with a five-card or longer major suit. These are forcing bids. Otherwise, bid 3NT. This is a signoff bid.

If the partnership uses Jacoby transfer bids in addition to the Stayman convention, responder can use the following guidelines for handling major suits[9]:

Number of cards in the major suit	Responder's Point Range		
	0–7 points	8 or 9 points	10–15 points
6 or more cards	Transfer & pass	Transfer & raise	Transfer & bid game
5 cards	Transfer & pass	Transfer & bid 2NT	Transfer & bid 3NT
4 cards	Pass	2♣ (Stayman)	2♣ (Stayman)
3 or fewer cards	Pass	2NT	3NT

Examples

Partner opens 1NT and the next player passes. What contract does responder want for the partnership with each of the following hands?

WEST	NORTH	EAST	SOUTH
	1NT	PASS	?

♠ J 5 3
♥ 6 3
♦ A Q 8 7 5
♣ K 8 2

3NT. With 10 high-card points plus 1 length point for the five-card suit, there is enough combined strength to take the partnership to game. With no interest in a major suit fit, raise to 3NT. There's no need to show the diamonds or be concerned about the low doubleton in hearts.

♠ 8
♥ 9 8 7 5 4 2
♦ J 6 3
♣ 8 4 2

2♥. With only 1 high-card point plus 2 length points for the six-card suit, the partnership belongs in partscore. Put the partnership in its eight-card fit. If the partnership uses Jacoby transfer bids, transfer to 2♥ and then pass.

---

[9] The partnership may also have methods for signing off or inviting with a minor suit , but that is outside the scope of this book.

♠ K J 8 6 5 3	4♠. There are 8 high-card points plus 2 length
♥ A 4	points for the six-card suit. That's enough to
♦ 6 5	put the partnership in game in the known
♣ 10 8 2	eight-card spade fit. If the partnership uses

transfer bids, transfer opener to spades and
raise to game.

Opening One-of-a-Suit

When a hand doesn't meet the requirements for a 1NT opening, the next priority is to consider opening the bidding in a suit at the one level. Opening bids of 1♣, 1♦, 1♥, and 1♠ cover a broad range of strength and hand patterns. They can be made with balanced hands outside the range for 1NT or with unbalanced hands.

Strength

The strength required for an opening bid of 1♣, 1♦, 1♥, or 1♠ is approximately 13-21 points. Hands with about 22 or more points are discussed in Chapter 4. When valuing the hand, the high-card points are typically added to the length points to determine whether there is enough to open at the one level.

Distribution

The best trump suit tends to be the one with the most cards in the combined partnership hands. Opener usually starts the bidding in the longest suit rather than the strongest. There are, however, exceptions.

FIVE-CARD MAJORS

A popular bidding style is to require that opener have at least five cards in a *major* suit to open 1♥ or 1♠. This *five-card major* approach is used throughout the book. With a choice between two five-card or six-card suits, open the higher-ranking.

MINOR SUIT OPENINGS

Hands with 13 or more points that don't meet the requirements for opening 1NT and don't have a five-card major are opened in the longer minor suit. Occasionally, this requires opening 1♣ or 1♦ with a three-card suit. This is often referred to as the *better minor* or, less appropriately, the *short club*. One piece of advice: don't cloud your thinking with visions of the 'short' club. Simply open in the longer minor suit. With four cards in both minors, open 1♦; with three cards in both minors, open 1♣.

Examples

The opponent on your right passes and you are in second position. What call would you make with each of the following hands?

WEST	NORTH	EAST	SOUTH
		PASS	?

♠ 4 2
♥ Q J 8 7 5
♦ A K 8 3
♣ K 4

1♥. There are 13 high-card points plus 1 length point for the five-card suit. Open the five-card major suit.

♠ A J 8 7 6 5
♥ K Q
♦ Q J 4 2
♣ A

1♠. This hand has 17 high-card points plus 2 length points for the six-card spade suit. An opening bid at the one level in a major suit shows a five-card or longer suit and any strength from about 13 to 21 points.

♠ K 9 8 7 5
♥ A Q J 6 2
♦ K J 3
♣ —

1♠. There are 14 high-card points plus 1 length point for each five-card suit, for a total of 16. With two five-card suits, open the higher-ranking.

♠ A K Q 2   1♦. Start with the longest suit. As the bidding
♥ 8   progresses, you'll have a chance to uncover a
♦ Q 9 8 7 5   spade fit, if there is one. The hand is worth
♣ A K J   20 points, 19 high-card points plus 1 length
               point for the five-card diamond suit.

♠ A 10 8 4   1♣. With no five-card major suit, open the
♥ K J 10 3   longer minor suit. On occasion, this will be
♦ 7 6   a three-card suit. With three cards in both
♣ K Q 4   minors, open 1♣.

♠ 3   1♦. There are 15 high-card points, but the
♥ A Q J 7   hand is unbalanced because of the singleton.
♦ K 10 8 3   With no five-card major and four cards in both
♣ K Q 7 6   minors, open 1♦.

The Guideline (Rule) of 20

If you open the bidding in first or second position, partner will expect a hand worth about 13 or more points and bid accordingly. For example, responder will take the partnership to at least the game level holding 13 or more points.

Some hands are borderline opening bids. Opener can use the following guideline[10] to decide whether to open at the one level in first or second position:

GUIDELINE OF 20

In borderline cases in first or second position, add the high-card points to the number of cards in the two longest suits. If the total is 20 or more, consider opening the bidding; otherwise pass.

---

[10] Although this is commonly called the Rule of 20, the term guideline is more accurate.

1) ♠ A J 7 5 3   2) ♠ A J 7 5
   ♥ K 4   ♥ K 4 3
   ♦ Q 10 7 3   ♦ Q 10 7 3
   ♣ J 5   ♣ J 5

Following this guideline, open the first hand (11 + 5 + 4 = 20) but not the second (11 + 4 + 4 = 19).

Examples

You are South. The player on your right has dealt and passed and you are in second position. What call would you make?

WEST	NORTH	EAST	SOUTH
		PASS	?

♠ 3
♥ A J 9 7
♦ K 10 8 3
♣ K J 7 6

1♦. There are only 12 high-card points, making this a borderline opening. Applying the Guideline of 20, add the high-card points to the number of cards in the two longest suits. It doesn't matter which suits you use when they are of equal length. That gives you 20 (12 + 4 + 4), enough to open. With four-cards in both minors, open 1♦.

♠ 3
♥ A J 8 7 5 3
♦ 9 5
♣ K Q 7 4

1♥. There are 10 high-card points plus 2 length points. With fewer than 13 points, this is a borderline opening bid. Using the Guideline of 20, you have enough to open 1♥ (10 + 6 + 4 = 20).

Responding to an Opening Bid of One-of-a-Suit

Since an opening bid of one-of-a-suit covers a much wider range of strength and distribution than an opening bid of 1NT, responder is not in a position to immediately decide How High and Where the partnership belongs. Instead, responder bids with about 6 or more points, giving opener an opportunity to further describe the strength and distribution of the hand.

Responder's choice of bid depends on whether the opening bid is in a major or a minor suit. When the opening bid is 1♥ or 1♠, responder's options in order of priority are:

- Raise opener's suit with support.[11]
- Bid a new suit.
- Bid notrump.

When the opening bid is 1♣ or 1♦, responder's priorities are:

- Bid a new suit.
- Bid notrump.
- Raise opener's suit with support.

The exact choice of response will depend on the partnership methods, but here are some examples.

Examples

You are South. Partner opens 1♥ and East passes. What would you respond with each of the following hands?

West	North	East	South
	1♥	Pass	?

---

[11] Responder might first bid a new suit or use some conventional bid such as Jacoby 2NT.

♠ 6 4
♥ K 7 5 2
♦ A Q J 3
♣ 9 6 5

3♥. With support, responder values the hand using *dummy points* in place of length points: 5 for a void, 3 for a singleton, 1 for a doubleton. This hand is worth 10 high-card points plus 1 point for the doubleton spade. A single raise would show about 6-10 points. With 11-12 points, responder makes an invitational jump raise—*limit raise*—to 3♥. With 13 or more, responder would get the partnership to the game level.

♠ K 9 8 5 3
♥ 6
♦ Q J 8 6 2
♣ 7 5

1♠. A new suit response at the one level shows 6 or more points and a four-card or longer suit. To bid a new suit at the two level, responder needs about 11 or more points[12]. With two five-card or longer suits, responder bids the higher-ranking.

♠ Q J 3
♥ 6 4
♦ Q 10 4
♣ K 8 7 6 3

1NT. With no support for opener's major, no suit bid at the one level, and not enough strength to bid a new suit at the two level, responder's only option with 6-10 points is to bid 1NT.

You are South. Partner opens 1♦ and East passes. What would you respond with each of the following hands?

WEST	NORTH	EAST	SOUTH
	1♦	PASS	?

♠ A J 8 4
♥ 6 2
♦ K J 7 6 2
♣ 9 3

1♠. Even with support for opener's diamonds, responder's priority is to look for a major suit fit by bidding a four-card or longer major at the one level.

---

[12] Some partnership methods require 13 or more points for a new suit at the two level.

♠ K 9 3
♥ Q 10 5
♦ Q 10 6
♣ A J 8 4

2NT. With no four-card or longer major, responder's second option after a minor suit opening with a balanced hand is to bid notrump. The partnership must agree on the range of responder's notrump bids. One popular style is to respond 1NT with 6-10 points, 2NT with 11-12, and 3NT with 13-15.

♠ A 9 3
♥ 7
♦ J 8 7 4 2
♣ Q 7 6 5

2♦. If responder can't bid a new suit and doesn't have a hand suitable for a notrump response, the last option is to raise opener's minor suit. In standard methods, a single raise shows about 6-10 points and a jump raise shows about 11-12 points. With 13 or more points, responder gets to game in notrump or the minor suit.

Improving Your Judgment

There's more to valuing a hand than adding the high-card and length points. Here are tips to help make better choices when you have borderline decisions.

1. Being Prepared

When you open the bidding in a suit in first or second position, responder's bid of a new suit is forcing, so you must be prepared to make a suitable rebid. With a minimum opening bid, you want to avoid making a *reverse*—bidding a new suit at the two level that is higher-ranking than your first suit. A reverse shows at least a medium-strength opening bid of about 17 or more points. This consideration can affect your choice of opening bid. For example, consider the following hands.

♠ 4
♥ K 7 3
♦ A K Q 8
♣ 9 6 5 3 2

If you open the longest suit, 1♣, you will have a difficult choice of rebid if partner responds 1♠. A rebid of 1NT would describe a balanced hand. A rebid of 2♦ would be a reverse, since diamonds are higher-ranking than clubs. Rebidding 2♣ with such a weak suit is also unsatisfactory. An option is to open 1♦ even though the clubs are longer. If partner responds 1♠, rebid 2♣, showing diamonds and clubs without promising extra strength. The disadvantage of this approach is that partner will assume the diamonds are as long as or longer than the clubs, but at least you get to show both suits.

♠ Q 5
♥ K J 7 3
♦ K Q 8 4 2
♣ K J

This hand presents a similar problem. You have 15 high-card points plus 1 point for the five-card suit. If you open 1♦ and partner responds 1♠, you aren't quite strong enough to reverse into 2♥. A 1NT rebid is also unsuitable because it describes a hand too weak to open 1NT, presumably fewer than 15 points. A rebid of 2♦ is possible, but partner will expect longer diamonds. A better option is to open 1NT, even though the hand is only *semi-balanced*, having more than one doubleton.

♠ A Q
♥ K J
♦ K 10 3
♣ Q 9 7 6 4 2

This hand is also semi-balanced. It's worth 17 points, 15 high-card points plus 2 length points for the six-card club suit. Opening 1NT again solves a potentially awkward rebid problem. If you open 1♣ and partner responds 1♥ or 1♠, a jump to 3♣ would show a medium-strength opening, but partner would expect a better suit. A rebid of 1NT would show fewer than 15 points, and a jump to 2NT would show 18 or 19 points. Open 1NT; it's an option, and it solves the rebid challenge.

2. The Intermediate Cards

High cards are the stars within each suit. The lower cards also have a role to play. Compare these two hands:

a) ♠ K 7 2
    ♥ A J 6
    ♦ K Q 4
    ♣ Q J 5 2

b) ♠ K 10 9
    ♥ A J 10
    ♦ K Q 10
    ♣ Q J 10 9

Both hands have 16 high-card points, and the high cards are in the same suits. Only the low cards are different, but the second hand feels much stronger.

Look at the club suit for example. In the first hand, you may not be able to develop club tricks if the missing high cards are unfavorably placed. In the second hand, you expect to promote two club tricks because the ♣10 and ♣9 accompany the ♣Q-J combination.

3. A Closer Look at Distribution

The distribution, or shape, of a hand can be important. The more unbalanced the hand, the more trick-taking potential. Compare these two hands:

a) ♠ K Q J
    ♥ A 10 9
    ♦ 10 9 4 3
    ♣ A Q J

b) ♠ K Q J 10 9
    ♥ A 4
    ♦ 3
    ♣ A Q J 10 9

The high cards are the same and there are the same low cards, but the second hand is much better than the first. In the first hand you expect to take two spades, a heart and two or three clubs—five or six tricks. In the second hand you expect to take four spades, one heart and four or five clubs—nine or ten tricks!

4. The Location of the High Cards

When honors are together in the same suit they have more trick-taking potential than when they are in separate suits. Compare these hands.

<pre>
a) ♠ K 9 8 5 3   b) ♠ A K Q 9 8
    ♥ A Q   ♥ 5 3
    ♦ Q 10 6   ♦ K Q 10
    ♣ K 7 2   ♣ 7 6 2
</pre>

Both hands have 14 high-card points and 1 distribution point. This might suggest they are equal in value. A closer look, focusing on where the high cards are located, tells a different story. On the first hand, the ♥A will take a trick. The other high cards may take tricks, depending on the position of the missing high cards.

On the second hand, there are three or more spade tricks and at least one diamond trick. There's much more trick-taking potential when high cards are working together in the same suit than when they are isolated in different suits.

Similarly, high cards in short suits don't always carry their full weight, especially if the partnership plays in a suit contract. A singleton king or a doubleton queen or jack may prove to be of little value. Consider these two suit combinations:

<pre>
a)   DUMMY   b)   DUMMY
      ♥ 10 9 6 2   ♥ 10 9 6 2

      DECLARER   DECLARER
      ♥ Q 5   ♥ 5 3
</pre>

In a suit contract, declarer has two heart losers in both combinations. The ♥Q is of no more value than a low heart. The queen would be more useful if it were located in another suit.

In a notrump contract, the ♥Q would have some value since it prevents the defenders from taking all the tricks in the suit. Dummy's ♥10 would become a winner in the first combination but not the second.

Now compare these two hands:

	a)			b)	
	♠	K		♠	3
	♥	A 9 6 4 3		♥	A K 9 6 4
	♦	Q J		♦	5 2
	♣	10 8 7 5 2		♣	Q J 10 8 7

The high cards and the low cards are the same and both hands satisfy the Guideline of 20 (10 + 5 + 5). The first hand, however, should be devalued because of the singleton ♠K and doubleton ♦Q and ♦J. Opener could pass. The second hand has no wasted high cards in short suits and could be opened 1♥.

SUMMARY

Opening the Bidding at the One Level in First or Second Position

Based on a style of five-card major suit opening bids, use the following guidelines for hands in the range of 13-21 points:

- Bid 1NT with a balanced hand and 15-17 points
  - even with a five-card major suit
  - even with a worthless doubleton

With a five-card or longer suit, bid the longer suit

- bid the higher-ranking of two five-card or six-card suits

Otherwise, bid the longer minor suit

- bid 1♦ with two four-card suits
- bid 1♣ with two three-card suits.

With Borderline Decisions

- In first and second position, use the Guideline of 20 with borderline hands. Add the high-card points to the number of cards in the two longest suits. If the total is 20 or more, consider opening the bidding; otherwise, pass.
- Be prepared to make a rebid, especially with a minimum hand. To avoid making a reverse, you can occasionally open the shorter of two suits. Also, semi-balanced hands can be opened 1NT if opening in a suit might lead to rebid problems.
- Be more aggressive when your high cards are working together, you have some intermediate cards, and you have long suits.
- Be more conservative when the high cards are in your short suits. A holding such as a singleton king or a doubleton queen doesn't carry its full weight.

Quiz – Part I

You are South and neither side is vulnerable. As the dealer, what call do you make with each of the following hands in first position?

WEST	NORTH	EAST	SOUTH
			?

a) ♠ J 4
   ♥ A J 3
   ♦ K J 7 6 2
   ♣ K Q 9

b) ♠ K Q 9 5 3
   ♥ 8
   ♦ A K 10 8 4
   ♣ K 6

c) ♠ J 7 5
   ♥ Q J 5 2
   ♦ K Q 7
   ♣ Q 9 5

d) ♠ A Q 8 7 3
   ♥ —
   ♦ 8 6
   ♣ A K 8 6 5 2

e) ♠ 10 8 7 5
   ♥ Q J 6 3
   ♦ A J 8
   ♣ A Q

f) ♠ 6
   ♥ A K 8 6
   ♦ 9 7 4
   ♣ K J 8 5 2

g) ♠ K J
   ♥ A 9 2
   ♦ A J 8 6
   ♣ K Q J 5

h) ♠ Q 10 7 5 3
   ♥ A 8 4 2
   ♦ K 7
   ♣ J 9

i) ♠ K J 10
   ♥ Q J 9
   ♦ A J 10 8 3
   ♣ Q 6

j) ♠ K 10 3
   ♥ K J 6
   ♦ A Q 10 8 4
   ♣ A 5

k) ♠ Q J 7 5
   ♥ A J 8
   ♦ A 9 2
   ♣ J 10 5

l) ♠ A J 9 7 5
   ♥ K 2
   ♦ Q J 8 4
   ♣ 7 2

m) ♠ A
   ♥ Q 9 7 5 3 2
   ♦ A K Q J
   ♣ Q J

n) ♠ K Q
   ♥ A K
   ♦ Q 10 7 5
   ♣ Q 10 8 6 3

o) ♠ Q 6 5 2
   ♥ K Q
   ♦ Q 7 3 2
   ♣ Q J 4

20

Answers to Quiz – Part I

a) **1NT**. This balanced hand with 15 high-card points plus 1 length point for the diamond suit meets the requirements for 1NT.

b) **1♠**. Open the higher-ranking of two five-card suits.

c) **Pass**. This hand doesn't qualify as an opening bid in first or second position using the Guideline of 20 (11 + 4 + 3 = 18).

d) **1♣**. Open the longer suit first, even with a five-card major.

e) **1♦**. Open the longer minor suit with a hand too weak for 1NT.

f) **1♣**. Qualifies as an opening bid under the Guideline of 20 (11 + 5 + 4 = 20).

g) **1♦**. Too strong for 1NT. With four cards in both minors, open 1♦.

h) **Pass**. The hand doesn't qualify under the Guideline of 20 (10 + 5 + 4 = 19).

i) **1NT**. 14 high-card points plus 1 for length qualifies for 1NT even if your range is 15-17.

j) **1♦**. 17 high-card points plus 1 length point is too much for 1NT.

k) **1♣**. With no five-card major, open 1♣ with three cards in each minor.

l) **1♠**. Qualifies as an opener using the Guideline of 20 (11 + 5 + 4 = 20).

m) **1♥**. 19 high-card plus 2 length points for the six-card heart suit put this hand at the top of the range for a 1♥ opening bid.

n) **1NT (1♣)**. There are 16 high-card points plus 1 length point for the five-card suit. In theory, that's enough strength to open the bidding 1♣ and reverse into 2♦ over a 1♥ or 1♠ response. In practice, with so little strength in the two long suits, a 1NT opening with this semi-balanced hand is a better description.

o) **Pass (1♦)**. With 12 high-card points, the hand does qualify for an opening bid of 1♦ when applying the Guideline of 20 (12 + 4 + 4 = 20). With so many queens and jacks and no intermediate cards, however, sound judgment would suggest passing.

Quiz – Part II

You are South and both sides are vulnerable. The dealer on your right passes. What call do you make with each of the following hands in second position?

WEST	NORTH	EAST	SOUTH
		PASS	?

a) ♠ K Q 9 5
  ♥ A J 10 7
  ♦ 4 3
  ♣ A Q 5

b) ♠ A Q
  ♥ K Q 5
  ♦ J 7 6 5 4 2
  ♣ K 9

c) ♠ A K 6 5
  ♥ A 4
  ♦ 9 7 6 3 2
  ♣ J 6

d) ♠ A 8 6
  ♥ K Q 9 3
  ♦ J 9
  ♣ Q 10 7 5

e) ♠ A 8 6
  ♥ K Q 9 3
  ♦ J 9 5
  ♣ Q 10 7

f) ♠ 4
  ♥ K J 9 8 7 3
  ♦ A J 10 5 4
  ♣ 8

g) ♠ K Q
  ♥ A Q
  ♦ J 8 6 3
  ♣ K 10 8 7 5

h) ♠ K Q 9 5
  ♥ K J 7 3
  ♦ 8 6 3
  ♣ A J

i) ♠ Q J 2
  ♥ K 9 7 3
  ♦ Q J 5
  ♣ Q J 4

j) ♠ K 7 5 3 2
  ♥ K
  ♦ A 9 7 6 2
  ♣ 8 3

k) ♠ A Q 8 5
  ♥ A K Q 5
  ♦ 4
  ♣ K Q J 7

l) ♠ 4
  ♥ A 8 3
  ♦ A K Q 10
  ♣ 7 5 4 3 2

m) ♠ K J
  ♥ K J 5
  ♦ J 9 7 6 5 2
  ♣ A Q

n) ♠ 9 4 2
  ♥ A 8 6 3
  ♦ A K Q
  ♣ 7 4 2

o) ♠ A K Q 4
  ♥ 10 8 7 5 3
  ♦ A 9 4
  ♣ 3

Answers to Quiz – Part II

a) 1NT. Don't worry about the low doubleton in diamonds.

b) 1NT. Treat the hand as balanced. If you open 1♦, you will have a difficult time showing the strength of the hand on the rebid.

c) 1♦. Longest suit first, even if it isn't the strongest.

d) 1♣. The hand satisfies the Guideline of 20 (12 + 4 + 4 = 20).

e) **Pass.** Move one card from the previous hand and it no longer qualifies as an opening bid (12 + 4 + 3 = 19).

f) 1♥. Only 9 high-card points but the Guideline of 20 is satisfied (9 + 6 + 5 = 20).

g) 1NT. Treat the hand as balanced to avoid rebid problems.

h) 1♦. An unpleasant choice of opening bid, but the five-card major style has some disadvantages.

i) **Pass.** Not enough to open, even using the Guideline of 20.

j) **Pass (1♠).** Devalue the strength because of the singleton ♥K and the absence of any 10's or 9's. It's a matter of judgment. Pass or 1♠ would be acceptable.

k) 1♣. 21 points, but still a one-level opening bid.

l) 1♦ (1♣). Treat the diamonds as a five-card suit. The rebid could be awkward if you open 1♣ and partner responds 1♠.

m) 1NT (1♦). There are 15 high-card points plus 2 length points for the six-card suit. The hand is only semi-balanced, but a 1NT opening bid is most descriptive. If you open 1♦, you may be faced with an awkward rebid if partner responds 1♥, for example. A rebid of 1NT or 2♦ would be an underbid; a jump to 2NT or to 3♦ with such a weak suit would be an overbid.

n) 1♣/1♦. With 13 high-card points and no five-card major, open in a minor suit. The guideline with three cards in both minors is to open 1♣ and no one would take issue with that. You are allowed to exercise some judgment, however, and opening 1♦ would certainly be acceptable here.

o) 1♥. An awkward hand in standard methods since you will be faced with a challenging rebid if partner responds 1NT or 2♣. Nonetheless, it's probably best to go with the five-card major suit rather than a 'prepared' 1♠.

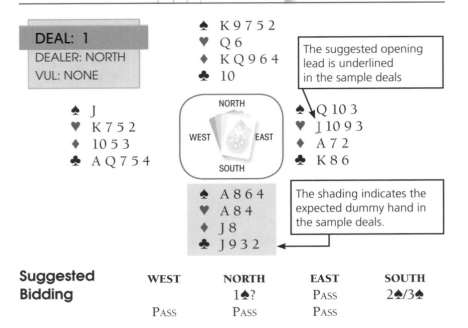

DEAL: 1
DEALER: NORTH
VUL: NONE

♠ K 9 7 5 2
♥ Q 6
♦ K Q 9 6 4
♣ 10

The suggested opening lead is underlined in the sample deals

♠ J
♥ K 7 5 2
♦ 10 5 3
♣ A Q 7 5 4

NORTH
WEST   EAST
SOUTH

♠ Q 10 3
♥ J 10 9 3
♦ A 7 2
♣ K 8 6

♠ A 8 6 4
♥ A 8 4
♦ J 8
♣ J 9 3 2

The shading indicates the expected dummy hand in the sample deals.

Suggested Bidding

WEST	NORTH	EAST	SOUTH
	1♠?	Pass	2♠/3♠
Pass	Pass	Pass	

The North hand has only 10 high-card and 2 length points. If North passes, the hand will likely be passed out, since none of the other players has a full opening bid. With a borderline hand, North might apply the Guideline of 20. With two five-card suits and 10 high-card points, the guideline suggests that the hand is worth an opening bid (10 + 5 + 5 = 20).

If North opens 1♠, South also has a judgment call to make. With 10 high-card points plus a doubleton diamond, the hand is on the borderline between a conservative raise to 2♠ and a more aggressive limit raise to 3♠. Whichever call South chooses, North should pass, having opened such a minimum hand.

Suggested Opening Lead

East has to make the opening lead and will likely choose the ♥J, top of the *solid sequence*.

Suggested Play

There's not much to the play on this hand. Declarer has four losers, one in each suit. If declarer plays a low heart from dummy on the opening lead, West will win the ♥K and probably play the ♣A (see below). Declarer still has to lose a trump trick—when the missing spades divide 3-1—and the ♦A. The missing diamonds divide 3-3, so declarer doesn't need to ruff any diamond losers in the dummy.

Suggested Defense

If East doesn't lead a heart initially, declarer could take ten tricks by driving out the ♦A and discarding dummy's two low hearts on the established diamond winners. Now declarer's heart loser can be ruffed in the dummy. So, the ♥J is the best opening lead for the defenders.

If East leads the ♥J and declarer plays a low heart from dummy, West wins the first trick with the ♥K. If West automatically returns partner's suit at trick two, declarer will win the ♥Q. Declarer can then use dummy's ♠A as an entry to play the ♥A and discard the ♣10. Declarer will take ten tricks, losing only one spade, one heart, and one diamond.

So, if North and South happen to reach game, East and West have to defend accurately to defeat the contract.

From the lead of the ♥J, West can infer that declarer holds the ♥Q, so there's not much future in hearts. West should probably switch to the ♣A, hoping to take any of the defenders' tricks in clubs before declarer can discard losers. If declarer holds the ♣K instead of East, no harm is done since declarer would be entitled to that trick sooner or later. On the actual deal, East holds the ♣K and should play the ♣8, an encouraging signal. The defenders, however, can get only one club trick because declarer has a singleton. The best they can do is get their ♦A and a trump trick to go along with the ♥K and ♣A. That holds declarer to nine tricks.

North's aggressive 1♠ opening bid gets the partnership to a successful partscore in spades.

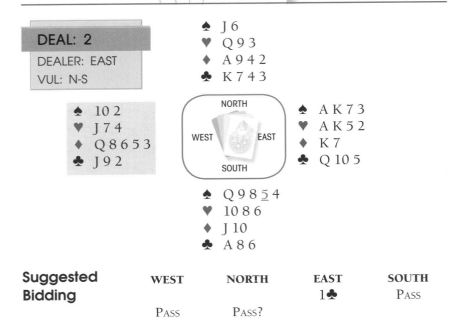

DEAL: 2

DEALER: EAST
VUL: N-S

NORTH
♠ J 6
♥ Q 9 3
♦ A 9 4 2
♣ K 7 4 3

WEST
♠ 10 2
♥ J 7 4
♦ Q 8 6 5 3
♣ J 9 2

EAST
♠ A K 7 3
♥ A K 5 2
♦ K 7
♣ Q 10 5

SOUTH
♠ Q 9 8 5 4
♥ 10 8 6
♦ J 10
♣ A 8 6

Suggested Bidding

WEST	NORTH	EAST	SOUTH
		1♣	PASS
PASS	PASS?		

East has a balanced hand with 19 high-card points—too strong to open 1NT but not strong enough for 2NT. With no five-card major, East opens the longer minor suit, 1♣. South's hand isn't good enough for an overcall, so the auction comes to West.

With only 4 high-card points plus 1 length point for the five-card suit, West doesn't have enough to respond. The 1♣ bid isn't forcing, so West should pass. Bidding is likely to get the partnership too high. If East has a minimum opening bid, the partnership may already be too high. If East has a strong hand, East's rebid will likely get the partnership overboard. On the actual hand, if West were to respond 1♦, East would jump to 2NT, taking the partnership beyond a safe level.

When the 1♣ bid is passed around to North, North should probably leave well enough alone and choose to defend 1♣. North could *balance* with 1NT, with less than the values for a 1NT opening bid, since South is marked with some strength when East–West stop at the one level. However, defending 1♣ is a reasonable choice.

Suggested Opening Lead

South has no clear-cut opening lead and will probably start with the ♠5, *fourth highest*, hoping to develop some tricks in spades. Leading a trump is another possibility.

Suggested Play

Low-level partscore contracts are difficult to play, especially on a three-three trump fit! In this situation, declarer should try to use the trumps separately to get more than one trick from the suit.

Unless the suits are breaking very badly—unlikely when the opponents have not entered the bidding—East can probably count on the ♠A–K and ♥A–K as four tricks. One trick can be promoted in the diamond suit and one trick can be promoted in the club suit, even though the defenders hold the ♣A and ♣K. Declarer needs to find one more trick. If South leads a spade, declarer can take two tricks with the ♠A and ♠K and lead a third spade, trumping in the dummy. Declarer must be careful to trump with a high club, not the ♣2, to avoid having North overruff with a low club.

Provided declarer ruffs the third round of spades with the ♣9 or ♣J, the contract can be made. If North doesn't overruff with the ♣K, East gets two spades, two hearts, one diamond, the spade ruff, and an eventual second trick in the club suit. If North does overruff with the ♣K, declarer can now promote two club winners by driving out South's ♣A.

Suggested Defense

There's no way to defeat the 1♣ contract even if the defenders find the best start of leading three rounds of clubs, removing all of declarer's trumps. Declarer can make the contract by establishing an extra trick in hearts since the missing hearts are divided 3-3.

Landing in a six-card trump fit after a 1♣ opening on a three-card suit can turn out to be a reasonable contract.

DEAL: 3	♠ Q J 4
DEALER: SOUTH	♥ 10 8 5 3
VUL: E-W	♦ A 6 4
	♣ 6 5 3

```
        ♠ A 9 6 2              NORTH                    ♠ 10 5 3
        ♥ K 9 4                                         ♥ J 7 6 2
        ♦ 8 7 2        WEST             EAST             ♦ J 3
        ♣ A 9 7                                         ♣ K 10 8 4
                               SOUTH
```

```
                    ♠ K 8 7
                    ♥ A Q
                    ♦ K Q 10 9 5
                    ♣ Q J 2
```

Suggested Bidding

WEST	NORTH	EAST	SOUTH
			1♦
Pass	1♥	Pass	2NT
Pass	3NT	Pass	Pass
Pass			

With a balanced hand of 17 high-card points plus 1 point for the five-card diamond suit, South is too strong to open 1NT if the partnership range is 15-17. Instead, South starts with 1♦.

West, with only 11 points, doesn't have the strength and distribution for a *takeout double*, so the bidding comes to North who responds 1♥, showing the four-card major suit.

East passes and South now finishes the description of the hand by jumping to 2NT, showing a balanced hand of 18-19 points. This isn't a forcing bid, but with 7 high-card points, North accepts the invitation and bids game. Even if the partnership has only 25 combined points, game should be a reasonable gamble.

Suggested Opening Lead

With no particular guidance from the auction, West will lead the ♠2, fourth highest from longest and strongest.

Suggested Play

Declarer starts with only four sure tricks, the ♥A and ♦A–K–Q. Provided the missing diamonds divide 3-2 or 4-1 with the ♦J singleton, declarer should get two more tricks from diamonds. The defenders have attacked spades, but declarer can get two spade tricks through promotion. One more trick is needed.

The heart finesse offers a 50% chance for a ninth trick—if East holds the ♥K. The club suit actually offers a 75% chance for the ninth trick. If East holds the ♣A or the ♣K or both, a trick can be developed by leading twice toward the ♣Q–J–2. Only if West holds both the ♣A and ♣K will this plan fail.

There is a danger that the defenders may be able to establish enough winners in spades to defeat the contract while declarer is developing a club trick, but this is very unlikely. West's lead of the ♠2, fourth highest, indicates that West holds only a four-card suit[13].

Declarer plays the ♠J on the first trick, hoping to win the trick in dummy. When the ♠J wins, declarer can lead a low club from dummy. If East plays low, South plays the ♣J, driving out West's ♣A. Assuming West continues leading spades, declarer can win a trick in dummy and lead another club toward the ♣Q. If East plays low, the ♣Q will immediately be the ninth trick. If East wins the ♣K, the ♣Q will be the ninth trick when declarer regains the lead.

Suggested Defense

If declarer finds the correct line of play, the defenders cannot defeat the contract unless East makes the unlikely play of winning an early trick with the ♣K and leading a heart. If East does find this play, North-South can offer their congratulations... and then find an easier pair of opponents!

If South were to open 1NT instead of 1♦, the auction might well end there. So, South's judgment on the opening bid could determine whether the hand is played in partscore or game.

---

[13] To prove this, try to construct a five-card or longer suit where the two is the fourth highest card. It can't be done.

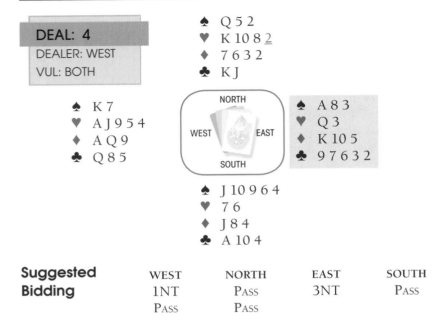

DEAL: 4
DEALER: WEST
VUL: BOTH

NORTH
♠ Q 5 2
♥ K 10 8 2
♦ 7 6 3 2
♣ K J

WEST
♠ K 7
♥ A J 9 5 4
♦ A Q 9
♣ Q 8 5

EAST
♠ A 8 3
♥ Q 3
♦ K 10 5
♣ 9 7 6 3 2

SOUTH
♠ J 10 9 6 4
♥ 7 6
♦ J 8 4
♣ A 10 4

Suggested	WEST	NORTH	EAST	SOUTH
Bidding	1NT	Pass	3NT	Pass
	Pass	Pass		

West has 16 high-card points plus 1 length point for the five-card suit. Although West has a five-card major suit, the hand falls into the range for a 1NT opening bid. This is more descriptive and avoids the challenge of having to describe the strength and distribution of the hand on the next round of bidding. For example, if West were to open 1♥, East would respond 1NT and West would have to choose between a conservative pass and an overbid of 2NT which would show 18 or 19 points...or make some other rebid that doesn't describe the hand.

North passes.

East has 9 high-card points plus 1 length point for the five-card suit. After West's 1NT opening, that's enough to take the partnership right to 3NT.

South, West, and North pass, ending the auction.

Suggested Opening Lead

North makes the opening lead. With no help from the auction, North would probably lead the ♥2, fourth highest from longest and strongest.

Suggested Play

Declarer, West, starts with two sure spade tricks, one heart, and three diamonds. Three more tricks are required. North's lead of the ♥2 presents declarer with an opportunity to develop all the extra tricks required from the heart suit.

The lead of the ♥2, fourth highest, not only gives declarer a trick in the suit that might otherwise be lost but also tells declarer that North has only a four-card heart suit. Declarer starts by playing dummy's ♥3 and wins the first trick with the ♥9. After winning the ♥9, declarer leads a low heart to dummy's ♥Q to drive out North's ♥K. If North wins this trick with the ♥K, declarer's remaining hearts are all winners. If North lets dummy's ♥Q win the second trick, declarer can return to the West hand with a high diamond to play the ♥A and another heart to North's ♥K. North gets only one heart trick and declarer gets four heart tricks. That's enough to make the contract.

Suggested Defense

If North leads a heart, the 3NT contract can no longer be defeated. North has to find a spade lead or a diamond lead to defeat the contract. Unless West bid hearts during the auction, however, North has no reason to lead a suit other than hearts.

If West chooses to open the bidding 1♥ instead of 1NT, East-West may not reach 3NT and, if they do, South is likely to be on lead and lead a spade, which would defeat the contract.

About Third Position
A hand should be opened in third position with a King less than the normal requirements, provided you have a fairly good suit.

—CHARLES GOREN, IN A NUTSHELL, 1946

About Fourth Position
It may be considered rather cautious bidding by some persons, but when in doubt there is nothing better than a new deal.

—R.F. FOSTER, FOSTER'S AUCTION MADE EASY, 1920

Opening at the One Level—
In Third and Fourth Position

The first step in valuing a hand is to look at the high-card points and distribution, but the process doesn't stop there. Your judgment, and results, will improve when you take other factors into account. The location of the high cards can make a difference; a king and queen working together in the same suit are often more valuable than a king in one suit and a queen in another. The lower-ranking cards can affect the value; 9's and 10's usually carry more weight than 2's and 3's. And then there's your position at the table.

If you are the dealer, in first position, partner has not yet bid. If the dealer on your right passes and you are in second position, the strength of partner's hand is also unknown. Bidding is a conversation, not a single statement, and you have certain obligations if you open the bidding in first or second position. Partner will expect a certain minimum amount of strength—typically 13 or more points—and will bid accordingly. If responder bids a new suit, it's *forcing*. Opener is expected to bid again. As a result, it's best to have sound values to open the bidding at the one level in first or second position.

The situation changes if you are in *third* or *fourth position*, sometimes referred to as *third* or *fourth chair* or *third* or *fourth seat*. Now you already know something about partner's hand; partner doesn't have enough for an opening bid. This can have an impact on the auction. One important point to keep in mind is that a new suit by responder is no longer forcing.

Let's see how this affects opener's thinking in third and fourth position.

Borderline Openings in Third Position

If both partner and the player on your right pass, you have an opportunity to open in third position. If you pass, the auction isn't over; the opponent on your left can still open. Since a new suit by responder, who is a passed hand, is no longer forcing, you don't have to be as concerned about making a rebid. This affects your strategy with a marginal hand. It's standard practice to open *light*, with less than the values for a first or second position opening bid.

Advantages of Opening Light in Third Position

There are several reasons for opening the bidding in third position when you have less than the values required for an opening bid in first or second seat.

MAKING A PARTSCORE

When partner has passed, the chance of making game is remote when you don't have a full opening bid. If neither partner ever opens with 11 or 12 points, however, your side will miss opportunities to make a partscore. These deals can add up over the long run.

HELPING PARTNER ON DEFENSE

If the opponents play the contract, your opening bid can help with the defense. It may get partner off to the best opening lead and help partner place the missing cards.

MAKING THINGS DIFFICULT FOR THE OPPONENTS

If the hand belongs to the opponents, your opening bid may get in their way, causing them to misjudge and bid too much or two little.

Valuing a Hand in Third Position

In third position, value the hand in the same manner as in first and second position, counting high-card points and length. With borderline hands, however, don't use the Guideline of 20. Instead, you can open a hand with as few as 9 or 10 high-card points, provided you are prepared to pass partner's response. If you do make a second bid, partner will expect a full opening bid.

Examples

As South, what call would you make with the following hands in third position after two passes, after partner and right-hand opponent pass?

West	North	East	South
	Pass	Pass	?

♠ A Q J 10 6
♥ 7 2
♦ Q J 4
♣ 7 4 3

1♠. You would probably choose to pass in first or second position since the hand doesn't qualify for an opening bid even using the Guideline of 20 (10 + 5 + 3 = 18). In third position, however, it may be worthwhile to open 1♠. You could make a partscore; you'll get partner off to the best lead if the opponents buy the contract; you may make it difficult for the opponents to find their best spot. If partner raises spades, bids 1NT, 2♣, 2♦, or 2♥, you can pass and play for partscore.

♠ 8 3
♥ 7 5 2
♦ Q 5 3
♣ A K Q 9 4

1♣. The hand isn't quite worth an opening bid in first or second position since it doesn't meet the Guideline of 20 (11 + 5 + 3 = 19). In third position, you can open a little lighter and you would certainly prefer a club lead if the opponents buy the contract.

♠ K 9 7 4
♥ Q J 6 3
♦ A J 8 4
♣ 5

1♦. The hand is borderline, but holding support for both major suits, it's probably worth opening light in third. If partner can bid a major or show support for diamonds, your side can likely make a partscore contract.

♠ Q 5
♥ K Q 9
♦ J 9 7 5 3
♣ A K 5

1NT. The requirements for opening 1NT don't change in third position. Partner will expect 15-17 points.

Borderline Openings in Fourth Position

Fourth position adds a new element to the equation. You have the same tactical considerations for opening light as in third position with the additional option of passing the hand out. If you pass, it's a 'tie' and neither side scores any points. If you choose to open the bidding, you want to be confident that your side will get a plus score for making a contract or for defeating the contract if the opponents win the auction.

There are 40 high-card points in the deck. If you have a borderline hand in fourth position, it's likely the missing points are fairly evenly divided among the other three players since none of them opened the bidding. Both sides will have a chance for a partscore and, when it comes to auctions in which both sides are likely to compete, the spade suit is critical. If both sides have a trump fit, the side that has a fit in spades has the advantage. To compete in any other suit, you have to go up a level, committing to take one more trick.

Valuing a Hand in Fourth Position—The Guideline (Rule) of 15

In fourth position, some players like to use a guideline developed by Don Pearson of Berkeley, California, commonly referred to as *Pearson Points* or the *Guideline*[14] *of 15*:

---

[14] This is usually referred to as the Rule of 15, but it is actually a guideline.

GUIDELINE OF 15

In borderline cases in fourth position, add the high-card points to the number of spades in the hand. If the total is 15 or more, consider opening the bidding; otherwise, consider passing.

WEST	NORTH	EAST	SOUTH
PASS	PASS	PASS	?

1) ♠ Q 8 5 2
     ♥ K 8 4
     ♦ 6
     ♣ A Q 7 3 2

2) ♠ 6
     ♥ K 8 4
     ♦ Q 8 5 2
     ♣ A Q 7 3 2

After three passes, the Guideline of 15 suggests opening the first hand (11 + 4 = 15) but passing the second (11 + 1 = 12), even though they are identical except for interchanging the spades and diamonds.

Examples

As South, what call would you make with these hands in fourth position after three passes?

WEST	NORTH	EAST	SOUTH
PASS	PASS	PASS	?

♠ K J 10 8 4
♥ J 7 3
♦ Q 7 5
♣ K J

1♠. This wouldn't be a sound opening in first or second position, but you can open light in third or fourth position with a good suit. It also satisfies the Guideline of 15 in fourth position (11 + 5 = 16). You can pass any response from partner, hoping for a small plus score.

♠ K 9 5
♥ Q 10 6
♦ J 9 4 3
♣ A 8 2

Pass. You would pass in any position with this hand. There's no need to get carried away with opening light when you have a poor hand. Take advantage of the opportunity to move on to the next deal.

♠ K 4
♥ A K J 8 5
♦ A Q J 8 3
♣ 7

1♥. Partner shouldn't expect you to have a light opening bid in fourth position. Most of the time, you will have full values. In this case, you have a near maximum, 18 high-card points plus 1 length point for each five-card suit.

♠ 8
♥ Q 3 2
♦ K Q 9 7 5
♣ A J 5 4

Pass. You would open this hand 1♦ in first, second, or third position. In fourth, however, it's probably best to pass. The hand does not satisfy the Guideline of 15 (12 + 1 = 13), so it's on with the next deal. If you open 1♦, the opponents are likely to compete in hearts or spades.

♠ Q 10 7 5
♥ 7 3
♦ A J 8 7 4
♣ A 5

1♦. This borderline opening bid meets the Guideline of 15 (11 + 4 = 15). Having made the decision to open, make the standard opening bid in your longest suit.

♠ K 7
♥ A Q 6 3
♦ K Q J 4
♣ Q 7 2

1NT. A 1NT opening bid shows 15-17 points in any position, including fourth.

The Effect of Vulnerability

Vulnerability is a term that was introduced by Harold Vanderbilt in 1925 when he introduced the modern form of scoring. In rubber bridge scoring, a partnership is non-vulnerable if it has not won a game[15]. A partnership becomes vulnerable after winning a game. The first partnership to win two games wins the rubber. In other forms of the game, such as Chicago scoring or duplicate bridge, vulnerability is simply assigned to each deal.

Vulnerability impacts the scoring. The bonus for making a vulnerable game or slam is greater than the bonus for making a non-vulnerable game or slam. The penalties for being defeated increase when the partnership is vulnerable, especially if the contract is doubled.

Vulnerability has no impact on opening bids at the one level when opener has 'full' values. It does become a factor, however, when deciding whether to open a borderline hand. Opener should take the vulnerability of both partnerships into consideration. There are three situations.

Equal Vulnerability

Equal vulnerability occurs when both partnerships are non vulnerable or both partnerships are vulnerable. In this situation, the potential risks and gains tend to balance out. For example, suppose both sides are vulnerable. If you open light and get too high, the penalty is greater, but if your light opening gets you to a game or a slam you would not otherwise have reached, there is more to gain.

Favorable Vulnerability

Favorable vulnerability occurs when your partnership is non-vulnerable and the opponents are vulnerable. In this situation,

---

[15] A game is won in rubber bridge by accumulating 100 or more points in trick score, either in a single deal or by combining two or more partscore deals.

the potential gains from bidding versus passing tend to outweigh the risks. If you get too high, the opponents may be able to make a vulnerable game or slam. Even if you are doubled, the penalty may not be as much as the value of the opponents' potential game or slam.

Unfavorable Vulnerability

Unfavorable vulnerability occurs when your partnership is vulnerable and the opponents are non-vulnerable. In this situation, the potential risks tend to outweigh the gains, so you should favor passing over opening. If you get too high and are doubled, the penalty can easily be larger than the value of the opponents' potential game or slam.

Responding to Opening Bids in Third and Fourth Position

If partner opens in third or fourth position, responder uses basically the same approach as responding to an opening bid in first or second position. Most of the time, opener will have full values for the opening bid and the auction will proceed in a manner similar to that following an opening bid in first or second position. There are, however, some things to keep in mind:

- Responder passed initially, so opener knows any response is limited to about 12 points. With 13 or more, responder would have opened the bidding. As a result, a new suit by responder is not forcing. Opener can pass with a minimum or light opening bid, knowing the partnership is unlikely to have enough combined strength for game.
- Responder should be aware that opener might not have the values expected for an opening bid in first or second position. Opener may have opened light, or with a four-card major suit, for example. With support for opener's suit, responder should be cautious about bidding a new suit, planning to show the

support on the next round. Since a new suit isn't forcing, responder may never get another chance. (See the Drury convention, page 45.)

- Although responder's hand will occasionally revalue to 13 or more points with support for opener's suit—counting dummy points—conventions such as *Jacoby 2NT* as a forcing raise in response to a major suit are of less value. It is designed to investigate slam possibilities, which become unlikely once responder passed initially. Most partnerships don't use such conventions when responder is a passed hand.

Examples

Neither side is vulnerable. As South, you pass as the dealer and partner, North, opens the bidding 1♦ in third position. What call do you make after East passes?

WEST	NORTH	EAST	SOUTH
			PASS
PASS	1♦	PASS	?

♠ A J 7 4
♥ K 10 7 5
♦ J 6 2
♣ 8 3

1♥. This is the same response you would make if partner opened 1♦ in first or second seat. Don't be surprised, however, if partner passes. Partner could have a light or minimum opening and be hoping to make a partscore.

♠ A 8 5
♥ 6 2
♦ K Q 8 7 4
♣ J 10 5

3♦. You have the values for a limit raise of opener's suit, so make the standard response. If partner has opened light, you could be too high but then the opponents can likely make something.

♠ 6 5
♥ A J 5
♦ 8 4
♣ Q 7 6 4 3 2

1NT. You don't have enough strength to respond in a new suit at the two level, so without a four-card or longer major or support for opener's suit, respond 1NT.

Your side is non-vulnerable and the opponents are vulnerable. As South, what call do you make as responder when after partner opens 1♥ in fourth position?

WEST	NORTH	EAST	SOUTH
		PASS	PASS
PASS	1♥	PASS	?

NORTH
WEST ♦ EAST
SOUTH

♠ 9 3
♥ 6 4
♦ A Q J 6 2
♣ K 7 6 5

2♦. You have enough strength to bid a new suit at the two level. Partner knows you don't have 13 or more points because of your initial pass. Partner will assume you have about 11-12 points and might decide to pass the response.

♠ K 10 5
♥ J 4
♦ J 6 5 3
♣ Q 7 4 3

1NT. This is the same response you would make after a 1♥ opening in first or second position[16].

♠ J 8 7 5 3
♥ K Q 4
♦ 6 2
♣ A 8 3

1♠ (3♥). With the strength for a limit raise but only three-card support, you usually bid a new suit, planning to support the major at the next opportunity. The risk here is that opener might pass the 1♠ response. It might be better to raise hearts right away...or adopt the Drury convention.

---

[16] If the partnership uses a forcing 1NT response to an opening bid of 1♥ or 1♠, it is no longer forcing once responder is a passed hand.

Improving Your Judgment

Here are tips to help you make better choices when opening the bidding in third or fourth position.

1. Keep the Goal in Mind

It's easy to fall into the trap of simply counting to 13 and then opening the bidding. A better approach is to keep the objective in mind. Compare these two hands:

a) ♠ A Q 10 7 6   b) ♠ 8 4
   ♥ J 9 3   ♥ J 9 3
   ♦ K 7 5   ♦ K 7 5
   ♣ 8 4   ♣ A Q 10 7 6

In first or second position, you shouldn't open either hand since the objective is to make a descriptive call that will serve as the basis for a constructive auction. Partner will expect a full opening bid.

In third position you might open either hand with the hope of getting a small partscore or helping partner on opening lead.

In fourth position, you want to get a plus score, or at least not get a minus score, which might happen if you open and get too high or the opponents compete and make a contract. That's a reason for applying the Guideline of 15 and opening with the first hand (10 + 5 = 15) but passing with the second hand (10 + 2 = 12).

2. Be Prepared for the Rebid

Opener should be prepared for any response and consider the possibility of having to find a rebid. Consider these two hands:

a) ♠ A J 10 7 5   b) ♠ A J 10 7 5
    ♥ Q 4   ♥ 4
    ♦ K 7 5   ♦ K 7 5
    ♣ J 8 3   ♣ Q 8 3 2

Both are borderline openings in third and fourth. To avoid getting too high with the first hand after opening 1♠, you are prepared to pass any response. Even if partner responds 2♥ you can pass since partner should have a five-card suit or longer to bid hearts at the two level.

On the second hand, however, you'll be awkwardly placed if you open 1♠ and partner responds 2♥. That might sway your judgment to pass rather than open.

3. Be Flexible with the Guidelines

When opening in first or second position, there are guidelines when you have a choice of suits to bid. In third and fourth position, you can occasionally consider bending the 'rules.' Look at these two hands:

a) ♠ Q 8 3   b) ♠ Q 8 3
    ♥ J 7 5 3   ♥ A K Q 10
    ♦ 9 4   ♦ 9 4
    ♣ A K Q 10   ♣ J 7 5 3

Both are borderline hands that are probably worth opening in third or fourth position. With the first hand, you'd make the standard opening bid of 1♣.

With the second hand, you might want to consider the advantage of opening 1♥ rather than 1♣, to suggest a lead if you don't win the auction. Even though the partnership style is five-card majors, there's always some room for judgment.

4. Drury

A disadvantage of light opening bids in third and fourth position is that responder is sometimes faced with a dilemma. Suppose you pass as South with this hand and partner opens the bidding 1♥. What call do you make?

WEST	NORTH	EAST	SOUTH
			PASS
PASS	1♥	PASS	?

♠ A J 4
♥ K 5 3
♦ Q 9 5 4 2
♣ 4 2

If partner opened in first or second position, you could respond 2♦, intending to later show the heart support. Now you can't afford to bid 2♦ since it is not forcing after your initial pass. If partner passes 2♦, you will have missed the heart fit. An invitational jump raise to 3♥ is not much better. You have only three-card support and you could get the partnership too high if partner has opened light. The partnership may have missed the opportunity to get a small plus score in a partscore contract of 2♥.

To get around this problem, some partnerships adopt the *Drury convention*. After an opening bid of 1♥ or 1♠ in third or fourth position, a response of 2♣ is artificial. It shows three-card or longer support for opener's suit with about 9 or more points and asks whether opener has a full opening bid. Using the popular style of *reverse Drury*, opener simply rebids the major suit with a light opening bid. Any other rebid shows interest in reaching game.

With this hand, you would respond with an artificial 2♣ to partner's 1♥ opening. If opener rebid 2♥, you would pass and settle for partscore.

SUMMARY

It is a good tactic to open light in third or fourth position, with as few as 9 or 10 high-card points. Since partner passed originally, a new suit response is not forcing. Vulnerability can be a consideration with borderline hands. In general opener tends to be more aggressive at favorable vulnerability and more conservative at unfavorable vulnerability.

Opening with Borderline Hands in Third Position

Requirement for opening light in third position:

- A good suit or willingness to pass partner's response.

Advantages of opening light in third position:

- To make a partscore contract.
- To find the best defense by suggesting a lead.
- To cause the opponents to misjudge the situation.

Opening with Borderline Hands in Fourth Position

Requirement for opening light in fourth position:

- Use the Guideline of 15. Add the high-card points to the number of spades. If the total is 15 or more, consider opening the bidding; otherwise, consider passing.

Advantage of opening light in fourth position:

- To get a plus score.

If the partnership frequently opens borderline hands in third and fourth position, it should consider using the Drury convention. After an opening bid of 1♥ or 1♠ in third or fourth position, a response of 2♣ is artificial and asks whether the opening bid is sound or light.

Quiz – Part I

You are South and neither side is vulnerable. Partner and the opponent on your right both pass. What call do you make with the following hands in third position?

WEST	NORTH	EAST	SOUTH
	PASS	PASS	?

NORTH
WEST EAST
SOUTH

a) ♠ K 9 8 6 3
♥ A Q J 9 5
♦ A
♣ 6 4

b) ♠ Q 7 6 4
♥ A K 10 9 3
♦ J 3
♣ 3 2

c) ♠ K Q 5
♥ Q 9 6 4
♦ K 9 7
♣ J 8 3

d) ♠ 9 7 3
♥ J 4
♦ A K J 10
♣ Q 7 3 2

e) ♠ 6 3
♥ K Q J 10
♦ 8 7 5 4 2
♣ A 3

f) ♠ Q J 7
♥ K Q J 10 5
♦ K 4
♣ A 10 9

g) ♠ Q 7
♥ Q 9 5
♦ K Q 7 2
♣ A J 8 3

h) ♠ J 9 7 5 2
♥ K J 3
♦ Q 9 5
♣ Q 7

i) ♠ 6 2
♥ A K 8 7
♦ K 3
♣ A K J 8 5

j) ♠ 7 3
♥ K 8 2
♦ 9 5
♣ A Q J 9 7 3

k) ♠ K 10 7 5
♥ Q J 9 8
♦ 8 3
♣ A J 5

l) ♠ A J 7 2
♥ K J 10 8 5
♦ 5
♣ 10 5 3

m) ♠ A K Q 7
♥ 8 6 2
♦ K J
♣ 8 5 3 2

n) ♠ A K J
♥ 9 7 5 3 2
♦ A K J 4
♣ 6

o) ♠ Q 7 2
♥ Q 8 3
♦ K Q J 9 4
♣ 5 3

Answers to Quiz – Part I

a) 1♠. A standard opening bid, the higher-ranking of two five-card suits.

b) 1♥. Only 10 high-card points, but worth a gamble in third position with the good heart suit.

c) **Pass.** Without a good suit, there's no reason to open light.

d) 1♦. A lead-directing bid.

e) **1♥ (Pass).** If you're going to open light, the honors in the heart suit are the main feature, and that's the suit you would want partner to lead on defense.

f) 1NT. A balanced hand in the 15-17 range.

g) 1♦. The standard opening bid. Don't open 1NT light in third or fourth position.

h) **Pass.** No reason to emphasize the weak spade suit.

i) 1♣. With a good hand, make the standard opening bid.

j) **1♣ (3♣).** Show the clubs. Some players might choose to open with a preemptive 3♣ in third position.

k) 1♣. With good support for both majors, it's probably worthwhile opening this hand.

l) **Pass (1♥).** You might risk opening this hand, but if partner responds 2♦ you will have an awkward rebid.

m) 1♠ (1♣). With a full opening bid of 13 high-card points, you would open 1♣ in first or second position since you don't have a five-card major suit. In third position, you would definitely open but might consider 1♠ instead of 1♣. If the opponents play the contract, you don't want a club lead from partner.

n) 1♥. Lead-directing considerations are not a factor when you have a sound opening bid and expect to win the auction. Start with the five-card major suit, as you would in any other position.

o) **1♦ (Pass).** Is it worth the risk to open 1♦ and get the partnership off to the best lead if your side is defending? A close decision. You are not vulnerable and are prepared to pass any response by partner, so many players would take a chance.

Quiz – Part II

You are South. Your side is vulnerable and the opponents are not. The dealer on your left passes and this is followed by two more passes. It's up to you in fourth position. What call do you make?

WEST	NORTH	EAST	SOUTH
PASS	PASS	PASS	?

a) ♠ A J 9 8
   ♥ 7
   ♦ A K 8 6 3
   ♣ K Q 5

b) ♠ J 8 5
   ♥ Q 9 7 6 3
   ♦ K 6 2
   ♣ Q 7

c) ♠ Q 10 7 5
   ♥ K 8
   ♦ Q 9 4
   ♣ A J 7 2

d) ♠ J 8
   ♥ K 9 7 6 5
   ♦ K J 8 4
   ♣ K 6

e) ♠ Q 10 4
   ♥ K 6
   ♦ A Q J 8 7
   ♣ K 9 2

f) ♠ 9 8 6 4 2
   ♥ K Q 7 4
   ♦ A J
   ♣ 9 8

g) ♠ A J
   ♥ K J 9 7 3
   ♦ K Q 5
   ♣ K 10 6

h) ♠ 3
   ♥ A J 8 3
   ♦ K J 10 2
   ♣ Q J 6 2

i) ♠ 7 5 4 2
   ♥ Q 9 7
   ♦ A 8 3
   ♣ K Q 5

j) ♠ 10 8 5
   ♥ A K Q 9
   ♦ K 8 3
   ♣ 7 5 4

k) ♠ —
   ♥ A K 9 5
   ♦ A Q 8 7 2
   ♣ Q 8 5 4

l) ♠ 9
   ♥ 3
   ♦ K Q 9 8 7 5
   ♣ A Q 8 7 3

m) ♠ K J 7 6 3
   ♥ 7 3
   ♦ A Q 8 6 3
   ♣ 4

n) ♠ A J 9 6 5 4
   ♥ A K Q
   ♦ 2
   ♣ K 9 4

o) ♠ J 8 7 5 2
   ♥ K
   ♦ K 7 6 4 2
   ♣ Q J

Answers to Quiz – Part II

a) **1♦**. Make the standard opening bid in the longest suit.

b) **Pass**. Not enough to open the bidding in any position.

c) **1♣**. A borderline opening, but it satisfies the Guideline of 15 (12 + 4 = 16).

d) **Pass**. A borderline hand that doesn't meet the Guideline of 15 (11 + 2 = 13).

e) **1NT**. Notrump opening bids are the same in all positions.

f) **1♠**. Only 10 high-card points, but it meets the Guideline of 15 (10 + 5 = 15).

g) **1♥**. Too strong for 1NT, 17 high-card points plus 1 for the five-card heart suit.

h) **Pass**. Too few spades to satisfy the Guideline of 15 (12 + 1 = 13).

i) **1♣**. The spades aren't great, but the Guideline of 15 is satisfied (11 + 4 = 15).

j) **1♥**. If you're going to open this hand in fourth, treat the hearts as a five-card suit.

k) **1♦**. The spade void shouldn't deter you from opening a good hand.

l) **Pass (3♦)**. The Guideline of 15 suggests passing, even though you'd open in any other position. If you want to open, a preemptive opening of 3♦ with only a six-card suit (or perhaps 2♦) might be better than 1♦. It would make it more difficult for the opponents to compete.

m) **1♠**. Only 10 high-card points but the hand does meet the Guideline of 15 (10 + 5 = 15).

n) **1♠**. A fourth position opening is made with strong hands, in addition to the occasional light opening.

o) **Pass (1♠)**. The hand does meet the Guideline of 15 (10 + 5 = 15), but that doesn't prevent you from exercising some judgment. All those queens and jacks and potentially wasted honors in short suits should persuade you to move on to the next deal.

DEAL: 5
DEALER: NORTH
VUL: NONE

♠ 10 9 8 4
♥ 7 5
♦ 9 7 2
♣ K 10 4 3

♠ K J 7
♥ A 8 6
♦ K Q 8 5
♣ A 6 2

NORTH

WEST   EAST

SOUTH

♠ Q 6 3
♥ 10 4 2
♦ A J 4 3
♣ Q J 8

♠ A 5 2
♥ K Q J 9 3
♦ 10 6
♣ 9 7 5

Suggested Bidding

WEST	NORTH	EAST	SOUTH
	PASS	PASS	1♥
1NT	PASS	3NT	PASS
PASS	PASS		

The South hand doesn't qualify as an opening bid in first or second position, even using the Guideline of 20 (10 + 5 + 3 = 18). With such a good heart suit, however, South might choose to open light in third position. North-South might buy the contract or push East-West too high or South's bid might get North off to the best opening lead.

On this hand, South's opening bid won't prevent West from overcalling 1NT, the same bid West would make if South passed. North has nothing to say, but East has enough to put the partnership in game in notrump, ending the auction.

Suggested Opening Lead

If South had not opened the bidding, North would lead the ♣3, fourth highest from the stronger four-card suit, or the ♠10, top of a sequence. South's 1♥ opening gives North useful information. North should now lead the ♥7, top of the doubleton in partner's suit.

Suggested Play

If North leads a heart, declarer can't make the contract. Declarer has only six sure tricks which can be taken without giving up the lead. A successful club finesse would provide only one extra trick, so declarer will eventually have to lead spades to try to promote two tricks. When declarer leads a spade, South can win the ♠A and take four established heart winners to defeat the contract.

It's a different result if North leads a club. Declarer can win the first trick with dummy's ♣J or ♣Q and immediately lead spades to promote two winners. It's too late for South to lead hearts. After the ♠A is driven out, declarer has two spade winners, the ♥A, four diamond tricks, and two club tricks.

If North leads a spade, declarer can still make the contract with careful play. Suppose South wins the ♠A and switches to a heart. West should hold up with the ♥A for two rounds, winning on the third round of the suit as North shows out. Now declarer can cross to dummy with a diamond winner to lead the ♣Q, taking the finesse. It doesn't matter that the finesse loses to North's ♣K. North is the safe opponent and has no hearts left to lead. Declarer again has two spades, one heart, four diamonds, and two club winners.

Suggested Defense

The only lead that allows the defenders to defeat the contract is a heart. Unless South opens the bidding 1♥ in third position, it's very unlikely that North will find the winning lead. With no clear-cut alternative, North should be sure to lead partner's suit if South does open 1♥. South's light opening has given enough information for the defenders to defeat the contract.

The tactical advantage of South's light opening in third position is that, if the opponents get to 3NT, North gets off to the best opening lead.

	♠ Q 10
DEAL: 6	♥ J 6 3
DEALER: EAST	♦ A Q J 8
VUL: N-S	♣ 10 7 6 3

♠ A 8 6 5 3	**NORTH**	♠ J 7
♥ 10 5 2		♥ A K Q 9 4
♦ K 7	**WEST** **EAST**	♦ 10 6 3
♣ A 8 5		♣ 9 4 2
	SOUTH	

♠ K 9 4 2
♥ 8 7
♦ 9 5 4 2
♣ K Q J

Suggested Bidding

WEST	NORTH	EAST	SOUTH
		PASS	PASS
1♠?	PASS	2♥	PASS
PASS	PASS		

After two passes, West might choose to open light in third position. The tactical advantages of this bid are that the partnership might be able to make a small partscore, the bid might get East off to the best opening lead on defense, or the opponents may misjudge the auction, bidding too much or too little.

If West does open 1♠, North passes and East will respond 2♥, under the assumption that West has a full opening bid. West, however, can now pass, settling for partscore. Since East passed originally, a new suit response is no longer forcing. If West were to bid again at this point, East would expect West to have a full opening and might then get the partnership too high.

Suggested Opening Lead

South is on lead against the 2♥ contract and will start with the ♣K, top of the solid three-card sequence.

Suggested Play

Assuming the missing hearts are divided 3-2, East still has a spade loser, three diamond losers, and two club losers, one too many. East could plan to lead toward the ♦K, hoping South has the ♦A, a 50% chance. A better plan is to ruff one of the diamond losers in the dummy after giving up two tricks in the suit.

East can't afford to combine both chances in the diamond suit. After winning the ♣A, declarer would have to use a trump to get to the East hand to try the diamond finesse. If that loses, the defenders could lead another round of trumps. Declarer can give up another diamond trick, but the defenders may be able to lead a third round of trumps, preventing declarer from ruffing the loser in dummy.

To be sure to get to ruff a diamond loser in dummy, declarer must lead a diamond right away after winning the ♣A. It seems unusual to lead a diamond away from the ♦K, but that is what declarer should do at trick two. If the defenders lead a trump, East wins and gives up a second diamond trick. The defenders can lead a second round of hearts, but East wins and still has a heart left in dummy to ruff the diamond loser. Declarer loses a spade, two diamonds, and two clubs, but makes the contract.

The ♦K is an optical illusion. It would be easier for declarer to lead a diamond at trick two if there were two low diamonds in the dummy.

Suggested Defense

It's unlikely that South will find the only opening lead to defeat the contract, a trump! It's quite possible, however, that the defenders will get a second chance if declarer crosses to the East hand with a high heart to try the diamond finesse. Now North must foresee the likelihood of a diamond ruff in dummy and should lead trump at every opportunity. There's no hurry to take the club winners. The defenders can win the race if declarer doesn't lead diamonds right away.

This hand could easily be passed out since no one at the table has a sound opening hand with 13 or more points. West's hand doesn't qualify as an opening bid in first or second position, but West can open light in third position, which gets the partnership to a partscore in hearts.

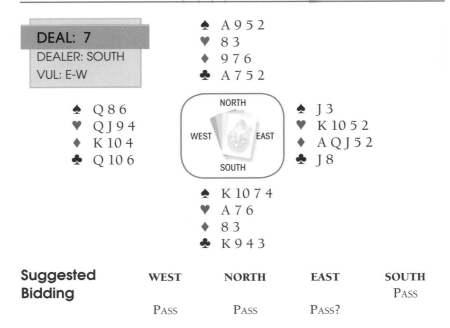

DEAL: 7
DEALER: SOUTH
VUL: E-W

North:
♠ A 9 5 2
♥ 8 3
♦ 9 7 6
♣ A 7 5 2

West:
♠ Q 8 6
♥ Q J 9 4
♦ K 10 4
♣ Q 10 6

East:
♠ J 3
♥ K 10 5 2
♦ A Q J 5 2
♣ J 8

South:
♠ K 10 7 4
♥ A 7 6
♦ 8 3
♣ K 9 4 3

Suggested Bidding

WEST	NORTH	EAST	SOUTH
			Pass
Pass	Pass	Pass?	

South doesn't have enough to open the bidding in first position and West doesn't have a sound opening bid in second position. North doesn't have enough for even a light opening bid in third position, so the auction should be passed all the way to East.

East has a hand that would be opened in first, second, or third position—12 high-card points plus 1 for the five-card suit. In fourth position, however, East should open the bidding on borderline hands only if there is a good chance of getting a plus score, either by making a contract or defeating the opponents if they compete. Otherwise, East is better off to pass.

The spade suit plays an important role in close decisions and East's hand doesn't qualify for an opening bid using the Guideline of 15 (12 high-card points + 2 spades = 14). The guideline suggests passing and moving on to the next deal.

If East does open 1♦, South might make a takeout double with support for the unbid suits. South has only 10 high-card points but North isn't going to expect too much since South passed originally. West may redouble to show 10 or more high-card points, or may simply respond 1♥. North may now bid 1♠. If East-West do reach 2♥ or 2♦, North-South might compete to 2♠. East-West will now have to decide whether to bid on the three level, where they are likely to be defeated.

The auction may not go that badly for East-West. North-South might not compete or might get too high, letting East-West get a plus score. This deal illustrates, however, the potential danger of opening a hand short in spades in fourth position.

Suggested Opening Lead

If East opens the bidding and North wins the contract in a spade partscore, East will be on lead and could choose the ♥2, low from four cards headed by an honor.

Suggested Play

In a spade contract, North has two potential spade losers, a heart loser, three diamond losers, and two potential club losers. If the five missing spades are divided 3-2, as might be expected, declarer will lose only one spade trick. Similarly, if the missing clubs are divided 3-2, there will be only one club loser. North can also plan to ruff a diamond loser in dummy. Declarer should finish with one spade loser, one heart loser, two diamond losers, and a club loser. North-South should make eight tricks in a spade contract.

If East-West play in a heart or a diamond partscore, declarer has to lose two spade tricks, a heart trick, and two club tricks. East-West can make eight tricks with either hearts or diamonds as the trump suit.

Suggested Defense

There's nothing East-West can do to prevent North-South from taking eight tricks in a spade contract. If North-South get to the three level, East-West should defeat the contract. Similarly, East-West can make eight tricks, but if they bid to the three level, North-South can defeat them.

If East opens the bidding in fourth position with 13 total points, it gives North-South an opportunity to get to a partscore of 2♠. Whether or not East-West compete to the three level, they are likely to finish with a minus score. The Guideline of 15 suggests that East pass with 12 high-card points and only two spades to minimize the risk of getting a minus score.

DEAL: 8	♠ Q 10 8 3
DEALER: WEST	♥ A 9 3 2
VUL: BOTH	♦ 6
	♣ K J 7 6

	NORTH	
♠ A 5		♠ K 4
♥ J 8 7 5	WEST ⬩ EAST	♥ Q 10 6
♦ K Q 5 2		♦ J 8 7 4 3
♣ 8 3 2	SOUTH	♣ A 10 4

♠ J 9 7 6 2
♥ K 4
♦ A 10 9
♣ Q 9 5

Suggested Bidding

WEST	NORTH	EAST	SOUTH
Pass	Pass	Pass	1♠?
Pass	3♠/4♠?	Pass	Pass
Pass			

None of the first three players really has enough to open. Even East, in third position, is unlikely to open light with such poor diamonds. That leaves everything up to South in fourth position. With only 10 high-card points, South may be tempted to pass and hope for a more exciting deal. If South always passes with such hands, however, the partnership is going to miss a lot of partscore opportunities in the long run. Despite the 10 high-card points, the Guideline of 15 suggests the South hand can be opened (10 high-card points + 5 spades = 15).

If South chooses to open 1♠, North, with the excellent spade support, can revalue the hand using dummy points. 10 high-card points plus 3 dummy points for the singleton diamond makes the hand worth 13 points.

Without conventional methods[17], it's difficult for North to describe such a strong hand opposite South's fourth-position opening bid. North

---

[17] If the partnership does use the Drury convention, North would respond 2♣ to ask whether South has opened light. South would rebid 2♠ (using the reverse Drury style) to show no interest in reaching game. North can still make one more try by raising to 3♠, but South will likely pass and the partnership will settle for partscore.

can't afford to bid a new suit, 2♣ for example, because a new suit by responder is no longer forcing once you are a passed hand. In fact, if North does respond 2♣, South is likely to pass to avoid getting the partnership overboard. So, North may have to settle for the underbid of a limit raise to 3♠, leaving some leeway if South opened light, or the overbid of 4♠, hoping South has a full opening bid or more.

Whatever North chooses to bid, that's likely to end the auction since South was never planning to get beyond partscore with this particular hand.

Suggested Opening Lead

Against a spade contract, West will probably start with the ♦K, top of the touching high cards.

Suggested Play

Declarer starts with two spade losers, two diamond losers, and a club loser. The hand plays nicely for declarer since the missing spades are divided 2-2 and both diamond losers can be trumped in the North hand. Declarer loses only the ♠A-K and the ♣A, making ten tricks.

If North-South reach game on these combined hands they should consider themselves very lucky since the hands fit together perfectly. The deal does illustrate, however, that you might want to think twice before tossing in the cards with the South hand when there are three passes to you.

Suggested Defense

East-West can do no better than take their three top tricks against a spade contract. They can consider themselves unlucky if North-South reach a game contract on these cards.

Using the Guideline of 15, South could open the bidding 1♠, even though South would pass in first or second position. This aggressive opening bid gets North-South to a successful partscore, or even game, in spades.

Ely Culbertson, the bridge authority in the 1930's, didn't believe that deceptive or obstructive bids belonged in the hands of the general public—although he was not above using such tactics himself! So, the weak two-bid came to an early end. Strong two-bids became the order of the day. In modern times, the weak two-bid is seen as part of standard bidding.

Obstructive Opening Bids

Obstructive bids are designed to get in the way of the opponents. They are popular in today's auctions. In addition to bidding *constructively* to your side's best contract, it's equally important to prevent the opponents from reaching their optimum spot. Bids that accomplish both objectives are especially useful and *preemptive opening bids*, or *preempts*, fall into that category.

Opening at a high level with less than the values for a one-level bid is risky. Yet, it's often a good idea. You could push the opponents too high; you could make your contract through a favorable lie of the cards; or you could be defeated but lose less than if the opponents were allowed to play in their best contract. On the other hand, the opponents could double you and get a good score. Preemptive opening bids require a delicate balance between aggressiveness and safety.

Playing Tricks

The value of a hand with a long suit is usually estimated using *playing tricks* instead of high-card and length points. Playing tricks are those you might reasonably expect to take if you buy the contract and name the trump suit. Compare these two hands:

1) ♠ A K 7   2) ♠ K Q J 10 9 8 7
   ♥ A K 9   ♥ 4
   ♦ A K 8   ♦ 10 3
   ♣ 8 7 6 4   ♣ 8 7 6

The first hand has 21 high-card points; the second has 6. Yet each is worth 6 playing tricks. There's no need to make an obstructive bid with the first hand. There's little chance the opponents will compete and you want to conserve the maximum bidding room to explore for the best contract. You might be able to make a game or slam in any of the four suits or in notrump.

The second hand, however, has little *defensive value* because you don't expect to take many tricks if the opponents win the contract and you are defending against a heart, diamond, or club contract. However, it has great *offensive value* if the hand is played with spades as the trump suit; you will be guaranteed to take six tricks. This is the ideal hand for a preemptive opening bid, describing the hand and obstructing the opponents.

When deciding whether to preempt and how high to preempt, it's helpful to estimate the number of playing tricks in the hand. This can be straightforward when there is a solid suit such as ♥Q-J-10-9-8-7-6. The ♥A and ♥K are missing, but once these cards are driven out, the remaining cards will be promoted into winners. There are five playing tricks in this suit.

In practice, the long suit is rarely solid. For example, you might hold a suit such as ♥A-Q-J-7-5-4-3. To estimate the playing tricks in a suit, assume the missing cards are divided as evenly as possible among the other three hands with the opponents holding any missing high cards. There are six missing cards, so you can assume each of the other players holds two cards. If you play the ♥A and then drive out the ♥K, the remaining hearts will be winners. That gives you six playing tricks from the suit.

This is only an estimate. The missing hearts might break badly, with a defender holding ♥K-10-9-8-6 and you could lose three tricks in the suit. You might not lose any tricks if partner holds the

♥K or if it is favorably located and you can reach partner's hand to take a finesse.

Holding the ♥J gives added protection. If an opponent holds ♥K-10-9, you still lose only one trick in the suit. If your holding was ♥A-7-6-5-4-3-2, you might still estimate six playing tricks under the assumption that the six missing hearts are divided 2-2-2, but you would feel less confident. If the missing hearts divide badly, the odds of being doubled for penalty increase. So, with a borderline decision, take the quality of the suit into consideration. You can be more aggressive holding the intermediate cards and less aggressive when they are missing.

Although the long suit is critical, side suits can contribute to the playing strength:

a)	♠ 7 6	b)	♠ K Q 10 7 5 4 2
	♥ 4		♥ 4
	♦ Q J 10 8 7 5 3		♦ 3
	♣ A 4 2		♣ 10 9 7 5

In the first hand, estimate five playing tricks from the diamond suit plus one from the ♣A, for a total of six tricks.

With the second hand, estimate seven playing tricks. The spade suit should provide six tricks if the missing spades are divided 2-2-2. The club suit could also provide a trick if the missing clubs are divided 3-3-3 around the table. You might do better or worse, but you have to make a reasonable estimate.

The Guideline (Rule) of 500

In making a preemptive opening, you deliberately overbid. You don't expect to make your contract unless partner can provide some tricks. If partner doesn't provide anything useful, you'll take only the tricks you started with and there's the possibility that the opponents could double the contract for penalties.

If you are defeated, it's likely the opponents could make something.

You don't have many defensive values outside your trump suit, and presumably partner couldn't provide a lot of tricks. It's relatively safe to make a preemptive opening provided the penalty for being doubled and defeated is no greater than the value of the opponents' potential contract. At worst, you break even. At best, your preemptive bid causes the opponents to misjudge the situation. They may double but not receive a large enough penalty to compensate for their game or slam; they may not double; they may bid too much, or too little.

To estimate how much you can afford to overbid, the guideline is to assume that the opponents can make a game contract. Although the value of an opponent's game depends on the vulnerability, the idea is that a game is worth approximately 500 points. So, you can overbid by two tricks when vulnerable since the penalty, if doubled, would be 500—200 for the first trick and 300 for the second. You can overbid by three tricks when non-vulnerable since the penalty would still be 500 if doubled—100 for the first trick, 200 for the second, and 200 for the third. This is called the *Guideline*[18] *of Two and Three* or the *Guideline of 500.*

GUIDELINE OF 500 (GUIDELINE OF TWO AND THREE)

When making a preemptive opening you can afford to:

- Overbid by two tricks when vulnerable.
- Overbid by three tricks when non-vulnerable.

Suppose you have six playing tricks and your side is non-vulnerable. You can afford to make a preemptive opening bid at the three level. At worst, you'll be doubled and defeated three tricks for a penalty of 500 points. If partner can provide a trick, the penalty will be only 300. If partner provides two tricks, the opponents may only be able to make a partscore, but the penalty will be 100 points and you'll still break about even. More likely, the preemptive opening will make it difficult for the opponents to get their optimal result on the deal.

---

[18] Usually referred to as the Rule of Two and Three or Rule of 500, although it is actually a guideline.

Openings at the Three Level or Higher

Opening suit bids at the three level or higher describe weak hands with a long suit. Estimating the number of playing tricks and applying the Guideline of 500 can be challenging, so the basic guidelines for opening a preemptive bid are often stated more simply, without taking playing tricks or vulnerability into consideration.

Three-Level Preemptive Openings

THREE-LEVEL PREEMPTIVE OPENING BIDS

An opening bid of 3♣, 3♦, 3♥, or 3♠ shows:
- a good seven-card suit
- less than the values for a one-level opening bid.

WEST	NORTH	EAST	SOUTH
			?

♠ 3
♥ K Q J 9 7 5 4
♦ 4 3
♣ 10 9 5

3♥. Following the guideline, this hand can be opened 3♥. There is a good seven-card suit and less than the values for an opening bid at the one level. The hand is ideal if you are non-vulnerable. There are six playing tricks, meeting the Guideline of 500—down three, or overbidding by three tricks. It would not be ideal when vulnerable because the Guideline of 500 would suggest overbidding by only two tricks. Nonetheless, most players would probably open 3♥ with this hand at any vulnerability.

♠ 6 5
♥ 2
♦ Q J 3
♣ A Q 10 9 7 5 4

3♣. This hand has a good seven-card suit and less than the values for a one-level opening bid. It illustrates the challenge in estimating playing tricks. The club suit will likely provide six tricks. Even if there is an unfavorable division of the clubs in the other three hands, it should provide at least five tricks. If the ♣K is favorably located, the club suit could provide seven tricks. The diamond suit might also provide a trick. On average, you could expect about seven playing tricks, making it ideal for a vulnerable three-level preemptive opening bid. Most players would open 3♣ regardless of the vulnerability.

Four-Level or Higher Preemptive Openings

> ### FOUR-LEVEL OR HIGHER PREEMPTIVE OPENING BIDS
> * With a weak hand and a good eight-card suit, open at the four level.
> * With a weak hand and a good nine-card suit, open at the game level in a major or a minor. at the game level in a major or minor.

WEST	NORTH	EAST	SOUTH
			?

♠ A K J 10 8 7 6 3
♥ 7
♦ 9 2
♣ 8 3

4♠. The guideline suggests opening this hand with 4♠. It is worth about eight playing tricks. Even though the ♠Q is missing, it can be expected to fall under the ♠A-K if the five missing spades are reasonably divided among the other hands. You are overbidding by two tricks. That would be in keeping with the Guideline of 500 if your side is vulnerable. If your side is non-vulnerable, you have one more trick than partner might expect. Nonetheless, it doesn't make any practical sense to open 5♠ since that would take the partnership beyond the game level. If partner can provide two tricks, you will make the contract.

♠ 9 4
♥ —
♦ K Q J 9 8 6 5 4 3
♣ 10 5

5♦. This hand is worth about eight playing tricks. If your side is non-vulnerable, overbidding by three tricks to 5♦ fits in with the Guideline of 500. Opening 5♦ when vulnerable is a little risky. Some players might make a more conservative choice of opening the bidding 4♦. Most players would open 5♦ anyway, relying on the potential gain from a high-level preemptive opening to outweigh the occasional 800-point penalty. It's a matter of partnership style.

Examples

You are the dealer and neither side is vulnerable. What call do you make with each of the following hands in first position?

WEST	NORTH	EAST	SOUTH
			?

♠ 4
♥ J 7 3
♦ A Q J 7 4 3 2
♣ 9 5

3♦. The hand has less than the values for an opening bid but there is a good seven-card suit. Open at the three level. If the hand belongs to the opponents, your bid should present them with a challenge. You expect to be defeated three tricks if partner has no help.

♠ Q 9 5
♥ Q 7 6 5 4 3 2
♦ 3
♣ Q 9

Pass. You have a seven-card heart suit but the suit is weak. It would be risky to open at the three level. There may be only four or five playing tricks.

♠ 10 8 2
♥ K Q J 8 7 5 4 3
♦ 5
♣ 6

4♥. With a weak hand and a good eight- card suit, open at the four level. That makes it difficult for the opponents to have a constructive auction if they have the majority of the strength. You are overbidding by three tricks.

♠ —
♥ 3
♦ 10 6 5
♣ K Q 10 9 7 5 4 3 2

5♣. With a nine-card suit, open at the game level. In a minor, that means opening at the five level. It might seem dangerous, but the more clubs you have, the worse your chance of taking any tricks on defense.

♠ K Q 10 9 7 5 4 3 2
♥ 3
♦ 10 6 5
♣ —

4♠. With a nine-card major suit, open at the game level. You don't want to go past game in case, with a little help from partner, you can take exactly 10 tricks.

Responding to Three-level or Higher Preemptive Opening Bids

A preemptive opening bid sends the message that opener has a long suit that will provide a lot of playing tricks provided that suit is trump. With no fit for opener's suit, responder should pass unless responder has enough strength to make a high-level contract with little or no help from opener. If responder does have enough strength to look for a game contract in a different trump suit, a new suit response below the game level is forcing.

When responder has a fit for opener's suit, the situation is different. There are two reasons for responder to consider bidding over opener's preempt. First, responder can have enough strength that the partnership belongs in game or slam. The contract will usually be played in opener's suit, but when opener's suit is clubs or diamonds, game in notrump becomes a possibility when responder has a fit and some strength in the other suits. Since the opening preemptive bid is essentially based on playing tricks, responder can estimate how high the partnership belongs by adding the number of playing tricks expected from opener to those in responder's hand. Playing tricks are more important than high-card points.

The second reason for bidding with a fit for opener's suit is that responder may want to take further preemptive action to try and keep the opponents out of the auction. Responder competes to the level of the number of combined trumps in the two hands. This is based on the *Law of Total Tricks*. Opener has shown little or no defensive strength outside the long suit. If responder also doesn't have many potential defensive tricks, the opponents are likely to have a game or slam contract. When responder has support for opener's long suit, even the aces and kings in that suit are unlikely to take tricks on defense. If, for example, opener has shown a seven-card suit and responder has four-card support, the opponents have only two cards in the suit. If they are divided 1-1, the opponents have only one loser; if they are divided 2-0, the opponents will have no losers in that suit when playing in a trump suit of their choosing.

RESPONDING TO A THREE-LEVEL PREEMPTIVE OPENING

- Responder focuses on the combined trick-taking potential of the hands.
- If the partnership is likely to have enough combined tricks for game, responder bids game.
- If the partnership is unlikely to have enough combined tricks for game, responder:
  - Passes with two or fewer trumps.
  - Raises with three or more trumps (preemptive).

Examples

You are South. The opponents are vulnerable and your side is not. Partner opens 3♥ and the next player passes. What would you respond with each of the following hands?

WEST	NORTH	EAST	SOUTH
	3♥	PASS	?

NORTH
WEST □ EAST
SOUTH

♠ K J 8 7 4
♥ —
♦ A J 8 6
♣ Q 9 4 2

Pass. Although you don't like partner's choice of trump suit, bidding will only get the partnership into more trouble. A new suit response would be forcing and partner's hand won't be of much value in a notrump contract.

If you pass, the opponents might bid and reach a poor contract.

♠ A K 7 5 2
♥ 6 4
♦ A K J 3
♣ 7 2

4♥. Partner has shown about six playing tricks with hearts as the trump suit with the non-vulnerable three-level preemptive opening. It looks like you can provide four tricks, so the partnership should go for the game bonus.

There's no need to mention the spades since there is a nine-card fit in hearts.

♠ 3
♥ Q 9 7
♦ 10 8 7 5 4
♣ K 6 3 2

4♥. With this hand, raise from weakness rather than strength. With a ten-card heart fit, you won't get more than one heart trick on defense since the three missing hearts can be divided 2-1 at best and might be 3-0 in the opponents' hands. There's not even a guarantee partner holds the ♥A. The opponents should be able to make at least game with spades as the trump suit, perhaps slam. Try to get in their way. If they double, the penalty won't be too large. Partner has about six playing tricks and partner might be able to trump one or two spade losers in the dummy or make use of the ♣K.

You are South. Both sides are vulnerable, partner opens 3♦ and the next player passes. What call do you make on each of the following hands?

WEST	NORTH	EAST	SOUTH
	3♦	PASS	?

♠ Q 9 7 4
♥ K Q 7 3
♦ 3
♣ K Q J 2

Pass. With not much of a fit, don't get the partnership any higher by bidding. Partner could have about seven playing tricks for the vulnerable 3♦ bid. You have enough that partner might just make the contract.

♠ A K Q 7 5
♥ A K J 6 3
♦ 4
♣ J 2

3♠. You have enough strength to try for a game contract even opposite a weak hand. A **3♠** response is forcing. If partner can't raise spades and bids 3NT or 4♦, try 4♥ next. Hopefully, the partnership can find its best spot.

♠ K 9 4
♥ A Q 6 5
♦ A 5
♣ K 10 7 2

3NT. Partner has shown a good seven-card suit, so with the ♦A and a low diamond to get to dummy you can hope to take seven diamond tricks to go with the ♥A. If the opponent on your left leads a spade, a heart, or a club, you should get a ninth trick. 3NT should be easier than 5♦.

The Weak Two-Bid

Weak two-bids are an extension of preemptive opening bids. They've been around since the 1930's but weren't incorporated in most early bidding systems. They were thought to be a gadget for experts only. Ely Culbertson, one of the first promoters of the game, felt that the general public wasn't ready for them, even though he used the weak two-bid himself. Charles Goren, in the 1950's, had the same reservation about introducing this tactic to his readers.

A 2♣ opening bid is reserved for all strong hands (see Chapter 4). The requirements for a weak two-bid are:

WEAK TWO-BIDS
An opening bid of 2♦, 2♥, or 2♠ shows:
- a good six-card suit
- 5-11 high-card points[19]

---

1)	♠ A K J 10 8 3	2)	♠ 8 6 5
	♥ 7 4		♥ Q J 8 7 4 2
	♦ Q 7 6		♦ Q 3
	♣ 9 2		♣ 8 5

The definition of 'good suit' is a matter of partnership style, vulnerability, and position at the table. The first hand would qualify as an opening 2♠ bid in most partnerships at any vulnerability in any position. You would expect to take at least five tricks with spades as the trump suit, perhaps six if the ♠Q is favorably located or you can make use of the ♦Q. So, it will fall within the Guideline of 500 even when your side is vulnerable.

Most players would not open the second hand 2♥, especially

---

[19] The popular high-card point range is 5-11. This can be confusing because 11 high-card points plus 2 points for length would be 13 combined points, enough for an opening bid at the one level. In fourth position, however, you would want to have about 11 high-card points to open a weak two-bid to be reasonably sure you will get a plus score.

when vulnerable. There are not enough playing tricks to meet the Guideline of 500. For a weak two-bid, most of the strength should be concentrated in the six-card suit, typically with two of the top three honors or three of the top five.

Examples

You are the dealer and neither side is vulnerable. What call do you make with each of the following hands in first position?

WEST	NORTH	EAST	SOUTH
			?

♠ 8 4
♥ K Q J 10 6 5
♦ K 9 5
♣ 7 3

2♥. With a good six-card suit and a hand that isn't strong enough to open at the one level, open a weak two-bid.

♠ A Q 10 9 6 2
♥ 4
♦ 6 4 2
♣ 10 8 3

2♠. There's no guarantee that you can take five playing tricks with spades as the trump suit, but the hand meets the general requirements for a weak two-bid: a good six-card suit and 5-11 points.

♠ 8 4
♥ 7
♦ Q J 10 9 7 5
♣ Q 10 6 2

2♦. This hand is on the low end of the scale but most players would risk a weak two-bid when non-vulnerable. The diamonds should provide four playing tricks and you will likely get one from the club suit. Overbidding by three tricks is in line with the Guideline of 500.

♠ 9 4 2
♥ A 7
♦ 6 4
♣ K J 10 8 6 5

Pass. This hand might qualify as a weak two-bid except that suit is clubs. The 2♣ opening bid is reserved for strong hands.

Responding to a Weak Two-Bid

Like preemptive opening bids at the three level or higher, the weak two-bid serves both as an obstructive bid and as an accurate description of the hand for responder. Responder can count on opener for about five playing tricks when non-vulnerable and about six playing tricks when vulnerable. Responder should focus on counting combined playing tricks rather than points when considering whether to bid or pass.

With a fit, responder can raise to game with four or five tricks and the expectation that the partnership will make the contract. Responder can also raise, however, as a further preemptive action. This can be effective because the opponents may be unsure which type of hand responder holds and whether or not to enter the auction.

A new suit is forcing. In addition, most partnerships treat a *2NT response* as artificial and forcing, asking for a further description of opener's hand when responder is interested in reaching a game contract. The partnership can use the following guidelines[20]:

RESPONDING TO A WEAK TWO-BID

Responder focuses on the combined trick-taking potential of the hands.
- If the partnership is likely to have enough combined tricks for game, responder bids game.
- If the partnership is unlikely to have enough combined tricks for game, responder:
  - Passes with two or fewer trumps.
  - Raises with three trumps (preemptive).
  - Raises to game with four or more trumps (preemptive).
- If unsure, responder can get more information by making a forcing bid:
  - A new suit below the game level.
  - 2NT (artificial)

---

[20] This is a popular set of agreements but some partnerships use other responses.

Examples

The opponents are vulnerable and your side is not. Partner opens
2♠ and the next player passes. What call do you make as South
with each of the following hands?

WEST	NORTH	EAST	SOUTH
	2♠	PASS	?

♠ 7 3
♥ K 8 5 2
♦ Q 9 6 2
♣ K 10 5

Pass. The partnership is likely to be too high already since partner only needs about five playing tricks to open with a non-vulnerable weak two-bid. The deal likely belongs to the opponents.

♠ 6
♥ K J 9 7 5 2
♦ K 8 3
♣ A J 2

Pass. With no fit for partner's suit, it is usually best to pass, even with the values for an opening bid or more. A response of 3♥ would be forcing and it's unlikely to get the partnership to a better contract.

♠ K 9 5
♥ 7
♦ A K J 7 3
♣ K Q 5 2

4♠. You can visualize partner taking about ten tricks. There should be six spade tricks, two diamonds, and a club and partner may be able to establish winners in the diamond suit or trump heart losers in your hand.

♠ Q 7 5 2
♥ 4
♦ K 9 8 6 3
♣ 9 8 2

4♠. Raise preemptively. It's likely the opponents can make a game or slam if given enough bidding room to find their best spot. You would jump to 4♠ even if the opponent on your right doubled or overcalled.

Both sides are vulnerable. North opens 2♦ and East passes. What call do you make as South with the following hands?

WEST	NORTH	EAST	SOUTH
	2♦	PASS	?

	NORTH	
WEST		EAST
	SOUTH	

♠ Q 3
♥ A Q 9 7 6 2
♦ 2
♣ A K J 4

2♥. The hand is strong enough to try for game even without a fit in opener's suit. The 2♥ response is forcing. If opener can show some support, you may make 4♥. If not, settle for partscore.

♠ A K J 4
♥ K Q 6 3
♦ K 6 2
♣ 7 2

2NT. You have enough strength to investigate a game contract. The 2NT response is artificial and forcing. If opener shows a feature in clubs, bid 3NT. If opener has a minimum, stop in 3♦.

OPENER'S REBID AFTER THE ARTIFICIAL 2NT RESPONSE

With a minimum (5-8): Rebid the long suit
With a maximum (9-11): Bid a side suit containing a feature such as an ace or king. Bid 3NT with no outside feature.

Improving Your Judgment

You don't have to open with a preemptive bid just because you have a long suit. It's an option. Your choice will depend on several factors. Experienced players use their judgment and imagination to enhance the guidelines.

1. Offense and Defense

For an ideal preempt, the high cards should be concentrated in the long suit, not the side suits. The hand then provides good offense in terms of playing tricks if you are declarer. The more high cards you have in other suits, the better your defensive values and the more tricks you can expect to take if the opponents play the hand. There is less likelihood the opponents can make anything. Compare these two hands:

a) ♠ A K J 10 8 4   b) ♠ K J 9 7 5 3
    ♥ 8 6   ♥ K 10 7 4
    ♦ 5 2   ♦ —
    ♣ 9 7 3   ♣ K 8 2

The first hand, with the concentrated strength in spades, is perfect for a weak 2♠ opening.

The second hand has more high-card strength but is less than ideal for 2♠. The partnership might belong in hearts, and there's defensive potential if the opponents come into the auction. Most players avoid opening a weak two-bid on hands with a four-card major suit on the side or with a void.

2. Position at the Table

When you are in first or second position, partner has not had a chance to make a call and could have a good hand. A preemptive opening should be sound since partner could have most of the missing strength.

In third position, you have more leeway. Partner has already passed, so you won't get in partner's way and the chance that the opponents have at least game has increased. This is the time to occasionally preempt with a poor suit or with one fewer cards than normal in your long suit.

In fourth position, there's no need to preempt the opponents since you can pass. Only open with a sound preempt, which you expect to make.

WEST	NORTH	EAST	SOUTH
PASS	PASS	PASS	?

a) ♠ 7
♥ J 9 8 6 5 4 3
♦ K 9 5
♣ J 8

b) ♠ A Q J 10 8 7 4
♥ 4
♦ J 10 7 3
♣ 3

The first hand wouldn't be a sound preempt in first or second seat with such a poor suit. In third, especially non-vulnerable, you might bend the rules and open 3♥.

The second hand would be a sound 3♠ preempt in first or second position. In third position, you might try putting extra pressure on the opponents by opening 4♠. In fourth position, you could open 3♠ since you can expect to make that contract if partner has a fair share of the missing strength and it will likely keep the opponents out of the auction.

3. The Guideline of 1, 2, and 3

The Guideline of 500, or Guideline of Two and Three, takes only your side's vulnerability into account. A loss of 500 points is a reasonable estimate of the value of the opponents' presumed game contract. A non-vulnerable game is worth about 400 points; a vulnerable game is worth about 600 points. A slight refinement is to consider the vulnerability of both sides when estimating the danger of overbidding.

1. **Unfavorable Vulnerability.** When your side is vulnerable and the opponents are not, you don't want to be defeated more than one trick. That would be a penalty of 200 points if doubled. If you are defeated two tricks, the penalty would be 500 points which is more than the value of the opponents' non-vulnerable game.

2. **Equal Vulnerability.** When both sides are not vulnerable, or both sides are vulnerable, you don't want to be defeated more than two tricks. If you are defeated two tricks doubled and non-vulnerable, the penalty is 300, less than the value of the opponents' non-vulnerable game. If you are defeated two tricks doubled and-vulnerable, the penalty is 500. That's okay if the opponents are also vulnerable since it is still less than the value of their game.

3. **Favorable vulnerability.** When the opponents are vulnerable and your side is not, you can afford to be defeated up to three tricks if doubled. The penalty would be 500 points, which would be less than the value of the opponents' vulnerable game.

This guideline is referred to as the *Guideline of One, Two, and Three*. It's a little more conservative guideline than the Guideline of 500.

4. The Guideline of Two, Three, and Four

In practice, preemptive opening bids are usually so effective that most partnerships adopt an approach that is more aggressive than the Guideline of 500, or the Guideline of One, Two, and Three:

Unfavorable Vulnerability	Bid for two tricks more than you have.
Equal Vulnerability	Bid for three tricks more than you have.
Favorable vulnerability	Bid for four tricks more than you have.

This approach, known as the *Guideline of Two, Three, and Four*, assumes that partner will provide at least one trick on most hands. If partner doesn't provide that trick and the opponents double, the penalty will be greater than the value of their potential game contract. This is a very small risk, however. Even when you have bid too much, the opponents don't always double and sometimes don't take all the tricks to which they are entitled when defending.

Consider this hand when the vulnerability is equal:

♠ K Q J 10 8 5
♥ 4
♦ 8 5 3
♣ 9 4 2

The hand has about five playing tricks and the Guideline of Two, Three, and Four would suggest opening 2♠ with this hand. That seems about right and is in line with both the guidelines for opening a weak two-bid and the Guideline of 500.

Suppose, however, that the vulnerability is favorable. The Guideline of Two, Three, and Four states that you can overbid by four more tricks that you have. That suggests opening 3♠ with this hand, rather than 2♠, even with the six-card suit. That might seem quite risky, but in today's game, the trend is toward taking a very aggressive approach to preemptive bidding. Some partnerships prefer a style that is even more aggressive.

In summary, the Guideline of Two, Three, and Four is the most aggressive style and could be described as 'light' preemptive opening bids in the partnership agreements. The Guideline of 500 is in the middle. The Guideline of One, Two, and Three is the most conservative style and could be described as 'sound'. Alternatively, you can ignore the vulnerability and simply open at the two level with a good six-card suit and at the three level with a good seven-card suit.

SUMMARY

Preemptive Opening Bids

A preemptive opening at the three level, 3♣, 3♦, 3♥, or 3♠ shows:
- A long, strong suit, typically seven cards in length.
- A weak hand, less than the values for a one-level opening bid.

With a longer suit, you can open at a higher level:
- With a weak hand and a good eight-card suit, open at the four level.
- With a weak hand and a good nine-card suit, open at the game level.

An opening bid of 2♦, 2♥, or 2♠ (2♣ is reserved for strong hands) shows:
- A good six-card suit;
- A weak hand, typically 5-11 high-card points.

The decision whether to open with a preemptive bid depends on:
- Partnership style
- Vulnerability
- Position at the table

The hand is usually evaluated in terms of playing tricks and the Guideline of 500 can be used as a guideline:
- Down two tricks vulnerable;
- Down three tricks non-vulnerable.

You tend be more aggressive at favorable vulnerability. You can also be more aggressive in third position, occasionally bidding with a weaker or shorter suit than would be required in first or second position. In fourth position, only make a preemptive opening bid if you expect to make the contract.

Responding to Preemptive Opening Bids

With support:
- With enough tricks for game, bid game.
- Otherwise bid to the level of the combined number of trumps.

Quiz – Part I

You are South and neither side is vulnerable. As the dealer, what call do you make with the following hands?

WEST	NORTH	EAST	SOUTH)
			?

a) ♠ 9 4
♥ 3
♦ 10 4 3
♣ K Q J 9 6 4 2

b) ♠ 6 3
♥ A K 10 9 7 3
♦ 10 9 6
♣ 8 4

c) ♠ J 8 6 5 4 3 2
♥ K Q 5
♦ 7
♣ Q 3

d) ♠ 6 3
♥ A K J 10 7 5 3 2
♦ 8
♣ 10 8

e) ♠ K J 4
♥ 3
♦ A Q J 9 7 5 2
♣ J 5

f) ♠ K Q 10 8 4 3
♥ 7
♦ Q J 5
♣ 9 4 2

g) ♠ —
♥ 6
♦ 7 6 3
♣ A K 10 9 8 7 5 3 2

h) ♠ Q 8 5 3
♥ A Q J 8 7 3
♦ —
♣ 9 4 2

i) ♠ 7 4
♥ K 9 5
♦ 8 2
♣ A J 10 8 4 2

You are South and both sides are vulnerable. The opponent on your right passes. What call do you make with the following hands in second position?

WEST	NORTH	EAST	SOUTH
		PASS	?

j) ♠ 5
♥ A K J 10 7 5
♦ J 10 6 2
♣ 7 3

k) ♠ 8 4
♥ 5
♦ A K Q 8 7 5 3
♣ 10 9 5

l) ♠ K J 9 7 4 3 2
♥ 8 6
♦ 7 4
♣ 4 2

Answers to Quiz – Part I

a) **3♣**. A good seven-card suit and only 6 high-card points, ideal for a non-vulnerable three-level preemptive opening. You can afford to overbid by three tricks, following the Guideline of 500.

b) **2♥**. With a good six-card suit you can open a weak two-bid.

c) **Pass**. With a poor suit and high cards outside of spades, this would not be a sound preemptive opening in any position.

d) **4♥**. With a good eight-card suit and no outside strength, open at the four level. This would be a good choice even if vulnerable.

e) **1♦**. You have a good seven-card suit and enough strength to open at the one level. No need to take away your side's bidding room.

f) **2♠**. An opening weak two-bid will describe the hand nicely: a good six-card suit and 5-11 points.

g) **5♣**. With a nine-card suit, open at the game level.

h) **Pass**. Most partnerships avoid weak two-bids with four-card support for an outside major or with a void. Here you have both.

i) **Pass**. You can't open a weak two-bid in clubs and the suit isn't long or strong enough for a three-level preempt in first or second position.

j) **2♥**. Although you are vulnerable, a weak two-bid should be relatively safe with this hand. You have at least five playing tricks in the heart suit and might take six if the ♥Q is favorably located. If not, you might get a sixth trick from the diamond suit.

k) **3♦**. The hand meets the requirements for a three-level preemptive opening bid. There are about seven playing tricks in diamonds unless the suit breaks badly, so vulnerability should not deter you.

l) **Pass**. You have a weak hand with a seven-card suit but it would be dangerous to open 3♠ when you are vulnerable. The suit isn't quite good enough, as there is no guarantee that you can take about seven tricks if the opponents were to double for penalty. Even a weak 2♠ opening would be a bit of a stretch with this hand. Partner will be expecting about 5-11 high-card points and a six-card suit. You have 4 high-card points and a seven-card suit.

Quiz – Part II

The opponents are vulnerable and you are not. What call do you make with the following hands after two passes to you in third position?

WEST	NORTH	EAST	SOUTH
	PASS	PASS	?

a) ♠ K J 10 9 7 4 3　　b) ♠ 8 3　　　　　c) ♠ 5
　♥ 7　　　　　　　　　♥ A K J 9 7 3　　♥ 10 3
　♦ J 9 3　　　　　　　♦ Q J 4　　　　　♦ J 9 6 4
　♣ 10 6　　　　　　　♣ 7 4　　　　　　♣ A K J 10 8 3

d) ♠ Q 5　　　　　　　e) ♠ Q 7 3　　　　f) ♠ A K J 10 7
　♥ 6　　　　　　　　　♥ Q 8 7 5 4 2　　♥ K 7 3
　♦ K Q 10 9 7 6 3 2　♦ K 5　　　　　　♦ 10 7 4
　♣ 5 2　　　　　　　　♣ 9 2　　　　　　♣ 9 4

g) ♠ 2　　　　　　　　h) ♠ 5　　　　　　i) ♠ K Q J 10 8
　♥ 7 5　　　　　　　　♥ A K Q 8 7 5 3　♥ 7 4
　♦ Q 10 9 7 6 5 3　　♦ 10 9 8 6　　　　♦ 10 3
　♣ 10 4 2　　　　　　♣ 9　　　　　　　♣ 9 7 4 2

Your side is vulnerable and the opponents are not. What call do you make with the following hands after three passes to you in fourth position?

WEST	NORTH	EAST	SOUTH
PASS	PASS	PASS	?

j) ♠ 9 4　　　　　　　k) ♠ J 8　　　　　l) ♠ A K Q 10 9 7
　♥ A K J 8 7 6　　　　♥ 10　　　　　　♥ 4
　♦ J 9 3　　　　　　　♦ K 6 2　　　　　♦ 6 4
　♣ 7 2　　　　　　　　♣ A J 9 7 5 4 3　♣ Q 10 7 3

Answers to Quiz – Part II

a) **3♠**. With a decent seven-card suit, open at the three level in third position. It would be a little riskier if your side were vulnerable.

b) **1♥/2♥**. You have enough to open at the one level, but in third position, you might choose a weak two-bid for tactical reasons.

c) **3♣**. You can't open a weak two-bid in clubs, but you might try a three-level preempt in third position with a good six-card suit.

d) **4♦**. A weak hand, a good eight-card suit, and partner has already passed. Time to put the maximum pressure on the opponents.

e) **Pass (2♥)**. Some players might open this hand with a weak two-bid in third position, but with such a poor suit, you could get into trouble.

f) **1♠**. This hand can be treated as a light opening bid in third position.

g) **3♦ (Pass)**. The suit isn't that great and you might suffer a large penalty. On the other hand, partner has passed, so the opponents very likely have a game or slam. Some players would take the risk of preempting.

h) **4♥ (3♥)**. Now that partner is a passed hand, opening 4♥ would be a reasonable shot. It might even make! In first or second position, partner would expect you to hold an eight-card suit.

i) **2♠ (Pass)**. You are in third position, non-vulnerable, opposite a passed partner. Perhaps this is the time to treat that five-card suit as a six-card suit.

j) **Pass**. A good weak two-bid, even vulnerable, in any position except fourth. You have the opportunity to pass the hand out, so don't give the opponents a chance to get back into the auction.

k) **Pass**. In addition to the fact that you are in fourth position and can pass the hand out, it would be dangerous to open a preemptive bid with this hand when your side is vulnerable and the opponents are not.

l) **2♠ (1♠)**. This hand is strong enough to open 1♠ but there's very little defense outside the spade suit. If you are ever going to open a weak two-bid in fourth position at unfavorable vulnerability, this is the time.

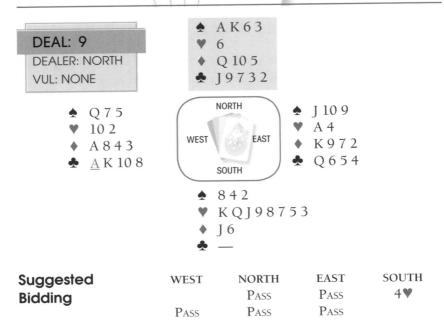

DEAL: 9
DEALER: NORTH
VUL: NONE

NORTH
♠ A K 6 3
♥ 6
♦ Q 10 5
♣ J 9 7 3 2

WEST
♠ Q 7 5
♥ 10 2
♦ A 8 4 3
♣ A K 10 8

EAST
♠ J 10 9
♥ A 4
♦ K 9 7 2
♣ Q 6 5 4

SOUTH
♠ 8 4 2
♥ K Q J 9 8 7 5 3
♦ J 6
♣ —

Suggested Bidding

WEST	NORTH	EAST	SOUTH
	PASS	PASS	4♥
PASS	PASS	PASS	

After two passes, the bidding comes to South in third position. South doesn't have enough to open at the one level but has a good heart suit that should be worth about seven playing tricks. With an eight-card suit, South can describe the hand with a preemptive opening of 4♥. That's in line with the Guideline of 500. Non-vulnerable, the worst that can happen is that South could be doubled and defeated three tricks for a penalty of 500 points. If partner's hand is also weak, East-West can likely make at least a game.

On this hand, the 4♥ bid is likely to buy the contract. West has enough to open at the one level, but not enough to come in at the four level, especially since partner has already passed. The meaning of a double by West is a matter of partnership style. Some partnerships would treat it as a *penalty double*; some would treat it as takeout; some as cooperative, showing enough high-card strength to likely defeat the contract but allowing partner to take out to a long suit with a good playing hand. On this deal, West may find that a double doesn't work very well, whatever the partnership agreement.

Suggested Opening Lead

West is on lead against the 4♥ contract and will start with the ♣A, top of the touching high cards.

Suggested Play

South has a spade loser, a heart loser, and two diamond losers. There's not much that can be done about the heart and diamond losers, so declarer should focus on eliminating the spade loser. Declarer's plan should be to promote a winner in the diamond suit by driving out the defenders' ♦A and ♦K.

After ruffing the opening club lead, South has to play diamonds before drawing trumps. The extra diamond winner must be established before the defenders can set up a spade winner. South should lead the ♦J. Either defender can win this trick and lead a spade, but declarer is a step ahead. Declarer can win and lead a high diamond to drive out the defenders' remaining high card. If they lead another spade, declarer wins in the North hand to play the established diamond winner and discard the spade loser from the South hand.

Now it's safe to start drawing trumps and give up the lead to the ♥A. Declarer loses only a heart and two diamond tricks.

Suggested Defense

If declarer ruffs the first club trick and immediately leads a trump, the defenders have a chance. East should win the ♥A and lead a spade. East can see that the defenders have no tricks coming from clubs and at most two tricks from diamonds. They will need to develop a spade winner. If declarer wins the spade and leads a diamond from dummy, the defender who wins this trick should lead another spade to establish a trick in the suit. When they later win a second diamond trick, they can take the spade winner to defeat the contract.

Of course, West could always defeat the contract by leading a spade initially, instead of a high club. Although that works on the actual deal, leading a high club would be the normal choice.

Preemptive openings make it difficult for the opponents to enter the auction.

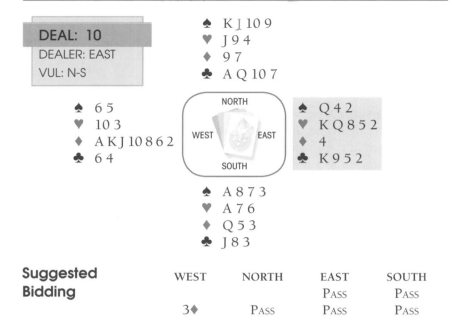

DEAL: 10
DEALER: EAST
VUL: N-S

North:
♠ K J 10 9
♥ J 9 4
♦ 9 7
♣ A Q 10 7

West:
♠ 6 5
♥ 10 3
♦ A K J 10 8 6 2
♣ 6 4

East:
♠ Q 4 2
♥ K Q 8 5 2
♦ 4
♣ K 9 5 2

South:
♠ A 8 7 3
♥ A 7 6
♦ Q 5 3
♣ J 8 3

Suggested Bidding

WEST	NORTH	EAST	SOUTH
		PASS	PASS
3♦	PASS	PASS	PASS

East doesn't have enough to open in first position, even using the Guideline of 20 (10 + 5 + 4 = 19). South also doesn't have enough to open. Non-vulnerable in third position, West has an ideal preemptive opening bid of 3♦. Not only does this describe the hand nicely to partner, it will also present a challenge to the opponents to get into the auction if the hand belongs to them.

North has support for the unbid suits but not enough strength to make a takeout double at the three level. East may not be happy with diamonds as the trump suit but should not attempt to 'improve' the contract. Any bid East makes could get the partnership to an inferior contract. Besides, West has described a hand that will only take a lot of tricks if the trump suit is diamonds. West has seven diamonds and East has one, so there's an eight-card fit.

South has 11 high-card points but the hand is unsuitable for a takeout double at the three level. South passes and the auction is over.

Suggested Opening Lead

Against the 3♦ contract, North could start with the ♠J, top of the interior sequence.

Suggested Play

West has two losers in spades, one in hearts, one in diamonds, and two in clubs. To make the contract, West will have to avoid a club loser and a diamond loser. To avoid the club loser, West can plan to lead toward dummy's ♣K, hoping North has the ♣A. With eight diamonds in the combined hands, the percentage play in diamonds is to take a finesse for the missing ♦Q rather than playing the ♦A-K hoping the ♦Q will fall. The guideline is eight ever, nine never: with eight combined cards missing the queen, take the finesse; with nine combined cards missing the queen, play the ace and king hoping the queen will fall. Because there is only one diamond in the East hand, declarer can't play the ♦A or ♦K before taking the finesse in case there is a singleton ♦Q.

To take the diamond finesse, declarer needs an entry to dummy. There is no immediate entry, so declarer will have to create an entry in hearts or clubs. If the defenders begin by leading three rounds of spades, West can ruff the third round and lead a heart to dummy's ♥Q. South can win the ♥A and the defenders can take a club winner, but they can't prevent declarer from regaining the lead and reaching dummy with the ♥K or ♣K. The ♦4 is led from dummy and, when South follows with a low diamond, declarer plays the ♦10 or ♦J, taking the finesse. When that works, declarer continues with the ♦A and ♦K. The ♦Q falls on the third round and West makes the contract.

Suggested Defense

On North's lead of the ♠J, South should play the ♠8 if a low spade is played from dummy. If North has the ♠K, the ♠J will win the trick. If West has the ♠K, declarer is entitled to one trick in the suit, and by playing an encouraging ♠8, South keeps dummy's ♠Q trapped and avoids giving declarer an extra trick in the suit.

When partner makes a preemptive bid, pass with no fit when game is unlikely. Partner's hand will provide few or no tricks if the long suit isn't trumps.

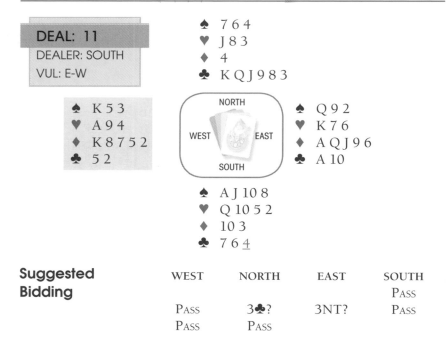

DEAL: 11
DEALER: SOUTH
VUL: E-W

North hand:
- ♠ 7 6 4
- ♥ J 8 3
- ♦ 4
- ♣ K Q J 9 8 3

West hand:
- ♠ K 5 3
- ♥ A 9 4
- ♦ K 8 7 5 2
- ♣ 5 2

East hand:
- ♠ Q 9 2
- ♥ K 7 6
- ♦ A Q J 9 6
- ♣ A 10

South hand:
- ♠ A J 10 8
- ♥ Q 10 5 2
- ♦ 10 3
- ♣ 7 6 4

Suggested Bidding

WEST	NORTH	EAST	SOUTH
			PASS
PASS	3♣?	3NT?	PASS
PASS	PASS		

After South and West pass, North has to decide what to do in third position. North doesn't have the right type of hand to open 1♣ and can't open 2♣, since that would show a strong hand.

An opening bid of 3♣ typically promises a seven-card suit. In third position, non-vulnerable, North can exercise some judgment. Partner has already passed, showing fewer than 13 points. Since North doesn't hold much in the way of high cards, it's quite likely that East-West have at least a game contract. Left to their own devices, they may well find their best spot. An opening preemptive bid of 3♣, however, could make their task more challenging. It's possible that the opponents might double and extract a large penalty, but the risk is worth taking.

If North passes, East and West have an easy time getting to their best spot. East opens 1NT and West raises to 3NT. If South leads anything except a club, that contract will make.

If, instead, North opens 3♣, East is faced with an uncomfortable choice. East might overcall 3♦, in which case the partnership might get to 5♦, which has little chance. East might make a takeout double, which is again likely to lead to a diamond contract. Or, East might overcall 3NT, hoping to find enough strength in the West hand to take nine tricks. That's probably the best choice, even though it doesn't prove successful on this particular hand.

Suggested Opening Lead

If North opens 3♣ and East becomes declarer in 3NT, South would have a difficult time justifying any lead other than a club. The lead from three low clubs in partner's suit depends on the partnership style. Some partnerships prefer a low club, some prefer *top of nothing*, some prefer the middle card, intending to follow with the top card, and then the low card—*MUD* (middle, up, down). Whatever the partnership style, a club lead works best for the defenders.

Suggested Play

In 3NT, East is unlikely to succeed after a club lead. East can hold up one round with the ♣A but will have to win the second round. There are only eight top tricks and a ninth trick can only come from the spade suit. Declarer might consider settling for eight tricks. However, it's usually best to try to make the contract even at the risk of going down an extra trick or two.

East can hope that North started with a seven-card club suit, leaving South with no more. East might try sneaking through a spade trick early by leading a low spade toward dummy, but South should hop up with the ♠A and lead another club to defeat the contract.

Suggested Defense

As long as South holds on to a club and takes the ♠A when given a chance, the defenders should be able to defeat 3NT. If East-West land in a diamond contract, the defenders can get two spade tricks, a heart trick and a club trick.

If North doesn't open the bidding, South would probably lead the ♠J, top of the interior sequence, against 3NT. That would allow East-West to take at least nine tricks, likely ten.

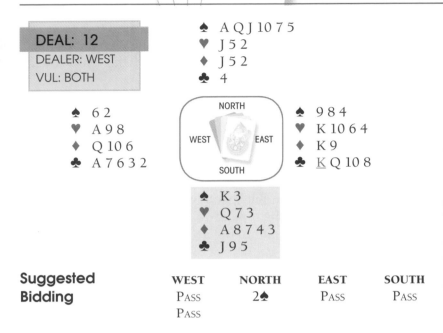

DEAL: 12
DEALER: WEST
VUL: BOTH

North hand:
- ♠ A Q J 10 7 5
- ♥ J 5 2
- ♦ J 5 2
- ♣ 4

West hand:
- ♠ 6 2
- ♥ A 9 8
- ♦ Q 10 6
- ♣ A 7 6 3 2

East hand:
- ♠ 9 8 4
- ♥ K 10 6 4
- ♦ K 9
- ♣ K Q 10 8

South hand:
- ♠ K 3
- ♥ Q 7 3
- ♦ A 8 7 4 3
- ♣ J 9 5

Suggested Bidding

WEST	NORTH	EAST	SOUTH
PASS	2♠	PASS	PASS
PASS			

After West passes, North doesn't have enough to open the bidding at the one level but North can describe the hand by opening 2♠.

On this deal, the 2♠ opening is likely to buy the contract. Neither East nor West has enough to enter the auction at the three level, even though East-West might make a partscore in clubs. South has no reason to bid any higher since North is showing about five playing tricks with spades as the trump suit and South can't contribute five more.

Suggested Opening Lead

Against a 2♠ contract, East would lead the ♣K, top of the *broken sequence*.

Suggested Play

In 2♠, there are three potential heart losers, two diamond losers, and a club loser. North could hope to avoid a heart loser by leading toward one of the honors, hoping a defender was dealt both the ♥A and ♥K. A better alternative, however, is to try to establish extra winners in the diamond suit on which to discard at least one heart loser.

Suppose the defenders lead two rounds of clubs. North can trump the second trick and play three rounds of spades to draw the missing trumps. Declarer should be careful not to discard a diamond from dummy on the third spade. Next, North leads a diamond, but plays low cards from both hands, giving up a trick to the defenders. Declarer can't afford to use dummy's ♦A too early, since it's the only sure entry to the dummy.

At this point, it won't do the defenders any good to take their ♥A and ♥K. If they do, they will make declarer's task easy, since the ♥Q will be established as a winner. Instead, they could lead another club. North ruffs, and again plays a low diamond from both hands, giving the defenders their second diamond trick. Now the defense has no winning play. If they lead a club, declarer can ruff, cross to dummy's ♦A, and play two more winning diamonds, discarding heart losers. Declarer will make an overtrick. If the defenders take their heart winners, they establish a heart trick for declarer, and the contract is still made.

Suggested Defense

The defenders cannot defeat the contract if declarer takes the recommended line of play. The best they can do is hold West to eight tricks. If declarer doesn't go after the diamonds, however, they have a chance. They should continue leading clubs, waiting for declarer to play the heart suit. If declarer leads hearts, the defenders can get three tricks in the suit and defeat the contract.

The heart suit on this hand is referred to as a frozen suit. Whoever breaks the ice by leading hearts gives up a trick to the other side. Recognizing frozen suits is important for both declarer and the defenders. Whether contracts are made or defeated will often depend on which side is forced to lead such a suit.

The weak two-bid is effective as both a constructive and an obstructive bid. It will often get the partnership to its best contract in one bid.

If you intend to pass your partner's forcing bid, it's best to drive to the bridge game in separate cars.

Strong
Opening Bids

Some hands have so much strength that they are likely to make game opposite little or no strength from partner. For example:

♠ 8
♥ A K Q J 8 6 5
♦ A 6
♣ A K 5

You can expect to take ten tricks with hearts as trump even if partner has no points and no hearts. If you open 1♥, there is the possibility that partner will pass and you'll miss a game. If you open 4♥, you haven't left much room to explore for slam. If partner has as little as the ♦K and ♣Q, you can take twelve tricks.

Such hands were traditionally opened with a *strong two-bid*, 2♥. This was forcing, so partner couldn't pass, and it left room to look for slam. With the advent of weak two-bids, however, opening bids of 2♦, 2♥, and 2♠ are no longer used to show strong hands. Instead, all strong hands of about 22 or more points are opened with an *artificial forcing 2♣*.

Examples

Both sides are vulnerable. What opening call would you make with each of the following hands?

WEST	NORTH	EAST	SOUTH
			?

NORTH

WEST   EAST

SOUTH

♠ A K 10 9 5 2
♥ A Q
♦ A K 9 4
♣ 6

2♣. There are only 20 high-card points but you can add 2 length points for the six-card spade suit. If you open 1♠, partner might pass and a game contract could be missed. Open 2♣, planning to rebid 2♠.

♠ K Q J
♥ A J
♦ K Q 7 3
♣ A Q J 4

2♣. Both balanced and unbalanced hands of 22 or more points are opened 2♣. This is a balanced hand with 23 high-card points.

Responding to a Strong Artificial 2♣ Opening

The opening 2♣ bid says nothing about clubs. It is merely an artificial forcing bid. Responder must bid something.

The Artificial 2♦ Response

The standard approach is for responder to make *a waiting response of 2♦*[21], leaving opener the maximum amount of room to describe the hand.

Suppose, for example, opener has a strong hand with hearts. Opener would start with 2♣. After responder bids 2♦, opener rebids 2♥. There's no need for opener to jump since the 2♥ rebid is also forcing. It's as though opener started with a strong two-bid in hearts.

---

[21] Some partnerships assign a different meaning to the responses to a strong 2♣ opening bid.

No extra room has been used when opener has a strong two-bid in a major suit. Only with a minor suit will opener have to show the "real" suit at the three level by rebidding 3♣ or 3♦.

Positive Response

With about 8 or more points, responder has the option of making an immediate *positive response* instead of the 2♦ response:

- A response of 2♥, 2♠, 3♣, or 3♦ shows a good five-card suit, typically with two of the top three honors, or a six-card or longer suit.
- A response of 2NT shows a balanced hand with about 8–11 points.

A positive response commits the partnership to the game level and shows interest in reaching a slam.

Examples

Neither side is vulnerable. North opens 2♣ and East passes. What do you respond as South with each of the following hands?

WEST	NORTH	EAST	SOUTH
	2♣	PASS	?

♠ J 8 5 4
♥ 8 7 6 2
♦ 8 3
♣ 6 4 2

2♦. Although you have only 1 point, you can't pass. The strength of opener's hand is unlimited and partner may not have any clubs. Make a 2♦ waiting response to leave room for opener to describe the nature of the hand.

♠ Q 9 7 6 5 4
♥ 6 3
♦ 7
♣ 9 8 6 3

2♦. The 2♦ response doesn't show a balanced hand or promise any length in diamonds. With this hand, you don't have the strength to make a positive response, so start with 2♦. You'll have an opportunity to show the long spade suit later.

♠ 4 2   2♥. With 9 high-card points and a five-card
♥ A Q 9 8 5   suit with two of the top three honors, you
♦ 7 5   have enough to make an immediate positive
♣ K 8 6 3   response of 2♥. You don't mind taking up
               some bidding room since the partnership is
headed for at least game and likely has enough for slam.

♠ 7 5   3♦. With a six-card or longer suit you don't
♥ 6 3   need two of the top three honors when
♦ K J 10 7 5 4 you have enough high-card strength for a
♣ A J 5   positive response. When the suit is diamonds,
               responder has to jump a level because the
2♦ response is artificial. Since you take away bidding room from
opener when making a positive response, responder has the option
of making a 2♦ waiting bid with this type of hand, planning to show
your suit later.

♠ K 8 7   2NT. With a balanced hand and 10 high-card
♥ Q 10 5   points, you can make an immediate positive
♦ Q J 7   response of 2NT. Many partnerships prefer to
♣ Q 9 6 4   specifically limit this response to about 8-11
               points with no aces. With more strength or
one or more aces, you would start with a 2♦ response and show
the extra strength after hearing opener's rebid.

♠ A 6 4   2♦. The 2♦ response doesn't necessarily show
♥ K 7 5 3   a weak hand. You may have a weak hand or
♦ 6   a hand unsuitable for a positive response.
♣ J 8 7 6 2   Although this hand has 8 high-card points,
               it isn't balanced and doesn't have a good five-
card suit. Start with the 2♦ waiting bid.

Responder's Negative Rebid

After responder's 2♦ waiting response, opener's rebid in a suit is forcing. Opener's strength is still unlimited, so responder must bid again. With a very weak hand—no aces or kings and fewer than 5 points—the classic agreement is that responder bids notrump at the cheapest level.

The disadvantage of this approach is that responder then becomes declarer if the partnership plays in 3NT. Opener's high cards will be put down in dummy, making it easier for the opponents to find the best defense. To avoid this, a popular approach is for responder to show a weak, or negative, hand by bidding the cheaper minor as follows:

- If opener rebids 2♥ or 2♠, 3♣ by responder is negative. A jump raise to 4♥ or 4♠ is also negative but shows four-card support.
- If opener rebids 3♣, 3♦ by responder is negative.
- If opener rebids 3♦, 3NT by responder is negative.[22]

This agreement is sometimes referred to as *cheaper minor second negative*. Any other rebid by responder commits the partnership to at least game. After making a negative rebid, a new suit by opener is still forcing but you can pass if opener simply rebids the same suit.

---

[22] This doesn't resolve the problem of having responder as declarer in a notrump contract but it's the best that can be done without resorting to more complex responses.

Examples

The opponents are vulnerable and you are not. North opens 2♣. As South, you respond 2♦ and partner rebids 2♥. What do you rebid with the following hands?

WEST	NORTH	EAST	SOUTH
	2♣	PASS	2♦
PASS	2♥	PASS	?

♠ 10 6 4 2
♥ 6 5
♦ Q 9 7 3
♣ 8 7 2

3♣. You can't pass, so you show a very weak hand by bidding the cheaper minor suit, 3♣. If the partnership doesn't have this agreement, rebid 2NT to show a weak hand. If opener rebids only 3♥, pass and stop short of game.

♠ 7 4
♥ K 7 2
♦ Q 8 6 5 2
♣ 7 6 2

3♥. You don't have much but you are too strong to make a negative rebid. The partnership should have enough combined strength for at least game and you can show the support for hearts.

Handling Strong Balanced Hands

Using the artificial 2♣ opening with strong hands of 22 or more points affects the ranges used for showing balanced hands. Here's the complete structure:

OPENING BALANCED HANDS	
0–11/12	Pass.
12/13–14	Open one-of-a-suit, planning to rebid notrump at the cheapest available level.
15–17	Open 1NT.
18–19	Open one-of-a-suit, planning to rebid notrump jumping a level.
20–21	Open 2NT.
22–24	Open 2♣, planning to rebid 2NT.
25–27	Open 2♣, planning to rebid 3NT.

An opening bid of 3NT is no longer needed to show a strong balanced hand. Instead, it can be assigned another meaning by the partnership.[23]

Examples

Neither side is vulnerable. As dealer, what is your opening bid with the following hands?

WEST	NORTH	EAST	SOUTH
			?

NORTH
WEST   EAST
SOUTH

♠ K J 8
♥ A Q 9
♦ K Q 7 5
♣ A J 6

2NT. With 20 high-card points, open 2NT showing a balanced hand of 20–21 points. This is not forcing and partner could pass.

[23] Some partnerships use an opening bid of 3NT to show a solid seven- or eight-card minor suit with very little outside strength. This is referred to as a *gambling 3NT*.

♠ A J 7 5
♥ K J 10 4
♦ A Q
♣ A K 10

2♣. With 22 high-card points, open 2♣. When responder bids 2♦, waiting to hear more about your hand, rebid 2NT showing a balanced hand of 22–24 points. This is not forcing and responder could pass with a very weak hand.

♠ A K 10 8
♥ K Q J
♦ A Q J
♣ A K 8

2♣. If partner responds 2♦, rebid 3NT, showing a balanced hand with 25–27 points.

The Subsequent Auction

After an opening bid of 2NT or opener's 2NT rebid following an opening bid of 2♣ and a 2♦ response, the partnership typically uses methods similar to those over a 1NT opening bid. 3♣ would be the Stayman convention, for example, asking opener to show a four-card major suit. If the partnership uses Jacoby transfer bids, a response of 3♦ would be a transfer to 3♥ and a response of 3♥ would be a transfer to 3♠[24].

Examples

Both sides are vulnerable. Partner opens 2NT. What is your response as South with the following hands?

West	North	East	South
	2NT	Pass	?

♠ J 9 7 3
♥ 7 2
♦ 8 6 4
♣ Q 8 6 5

Pass. The opening bid of 2NT shows at most 21 points. It's unlikely the partnership has enough combined strength for a game contract.

---

[24] After a 3NT rebid, the partnership can agree to use 4♣ as the Stayman convention and 4♦ and 4♥ as transfer bids.

♠ Q 4
♥ J 8 2
♦ K 6 4 3 2
♣ 7 5 3

3NT. With 6 high-card points plus 1 length point for the five-card suit, you have enough to take the partnership to game. There's no need to mention the diamond suit.

♠ 7 5
♥ Q 10 7 6 4
♦ A 6 3
♣ 7 4 2

3♦ (3♥). If the partnership uses Jacoby transfer bids, you would respond 3♦ as a transfer to 3♥ and then bid 3NT, asking opener to choose between 3NT and 4♥. If you do not use transfer bids, make a forcing response of 3♥, asking opener to choose between 3NT and 4♥.

You are vulnerable and the opponents are not. Partner opens 2♣. You respond 2♦ and partner rebids 2NT. As South, what is your next bid with the following hands?

West	North	East	South
	2♣	Pass	2♦
Pass	2NT	Pass	?

♠ 8 6 4
♥ 10 7 3
♦ 8 6 4
♣ J 7 5 2

Pass. Opener's 2NT rebid is not forcing. You have so little strength that game is unlikely. Settle for partscore.

♠ Q 10 7 5
♥ 6 2
♦ Q 9 7 3
♣ 8 4 2

3♣. The partnership should have enough strength for game since opener has at least 22 points. You can check for an eight-card major using the Stayman convention. If opener bids 3♠, raise to 4♠. If opener bids 3♦ or 3♥, bid 3NT.

♠ J 8 7 5 4 2
♥ 3
♦ 9 4
♣ Q 7 6 2

3♥ (4♠). If the partnership uses Jacoby transfer bids, respond 3♥ to transfer to spades and then raise to game. The partnership must have an eight-card fit since opener is showing a balanced hand. If the partnership doesn't use transfer bids, simply jump to 4♠. You have 3 high-card points plus 2 length points for the six-card suit. That should be enough to go for a game contract opposite 22-24 points.

Handling Strong Unbalanced Hands

If opener rebids a suit rather than notrump after opening 2♣, that is still a forcing bid. The style for some partnerships is that the auction must then continue until at least game is reached. A more common agreement is that, if responder makes a negative rebid and opener merely rebids the long suit, responder can pass. If opener shows a second suit, responder must keep the bidding going to at least game.

♠ A Q 9 ♥ A K Q J 8 5 ♦ K Q 6 ♣ J	You open 2♣ and responder bids 2♦. You now show the strong two-bid in hearts by bidding 2♥. If responder now makes a negative rebid[25], rebid 3♥. This isn't forcing and responder can pass with a very weak hand.
♠ A K J 9 6 ♥ A K Q 8 2 ♦ 3 ♣ A J	You open 2♣ and get a 2♦ waiting response from partner. The guidelines with a choice of suits to bid are the same as when opening at the one level. Rebid 2♠, the higher-ranking of the two five-card suits. If responder makes

a negative rebid, show the second suit by bidding 3♥. Responder can't pass this bid, even with no points, since the partnership is now committed to the game level.

If responder makes a positive bid, either immediately in response to the 2♣ opening or after hearing opener's rebid, the partnership is committed to the game level. If responder raises opener's suit, for

---

[25] 2NT, or 3♣ if the partnership uses the cheaper minor as responder's second negative.

example, the partnership is headed for at least game and perhaps a slam. Once the trump suit has been agreed, the partnership's normal slam bidding methods, such as Blackwood and cue-bids, come into effect.

Since a simple raise of opener's suit is forcing and shows some values, responder can show support for opener's suit with a very weak hand by jumping directly to the game level. On the first hand above, for example, responder's jump to 4♥ over opener's 2♥ rebid would say, "I have support for your hearts but nothing else that would be of any value... no ace, no king, no singleton, and no void. If you want to bid slam you're on your own."

Examples

As South, what opening call would you make with each of the following hands with neither side vulnerable? What do you plan to do next?

West	North	East	South
			?

♠ A Q
♥ A K Q 9 8
♦ 3
♣ A K J 10 5

2♣. If partner responds 2♦, plan to rebid 2♥, showing a strong two-bid in hearts. If partner makes a negative rebid of 3♣, show the second suit by bidding 4♣[26]. That's forcing and the next move is up to partner.

♠ A Q J 9 8 3
♥ Q
♦ A Q J
♣ A Q 5

2♣. If partner responds 2♦, rebid 2♠ to show the strong two-bid. If partner then makes a negative rebid, bid 3♠. This is not forcing, so partner can pass with nothing of value.

---

[26] If the partnership uses a rebid of 2NT by responder as the negative rebid, opener can bid 3♣ to show the second suit.

♠ Q 4　　　　　2♣. If partner responds 2♦, rebid 3♦, showing
♥ A K J　　　　a strong 'two-bid' in diamonds. A disadvantage
♦ A K J 9 8 7 3　of the artificial 2♣ opening is that you can't
♣ A　　　　　　show your minor suit below the three level.

Improving Your Judgment

The guideline for opening 2♣ is about 22 or more points. However, other factors can affect the decision on whether to open 2♣.

1. Offensive Tricks

An unbalanced hand should have good playing-trick potential to be opened 2♣. Ideally, you should be within one trick of game. Consider these two hands:

a) ♠ A Q 8 4　　　　　b) ♠ A K Q 10 9 3
　 ♥ Q　　　　　　　　　 ♥ A K Q 4
　 ♦ A K Q　　　　　　　 ♦ 3
　 ♣ A J 8 4 3　　　　　 ♣ 4 2

The first hand has 22 high-card points plus 1 length point. There are only five sure tricks, however, and it wouldn't be a good idea to open 2♣. If partner bids 2♦, you don't want to rebid 3♣ with such a meager suit. Open 1♣. If partner can't respond over that, it's unlikely your side has a game.

The second hand has only 18 high-card points plus 2 length points for the six-card suit, but it's a much better hand to open 2♣. If the missing spades and hearts are reasonably evenly divided among the other three hands, you can likely take ten tricks with no high-card help from partner.

2. Defensive Tricks

To open 2♣, you should have some aces and kings that will take tricks even if you are defending. Compare these hands:

a)	♠ A	b)	♠ —
	♥ A K Q J 10 8		♥ K Q J 10 8 7 6 5
	♦ A K 8 4		♦ Q J 10 9 7
	♣ K Q		♣ —

The first hand has offensive potential and should produce at least 10 tricks with hearts as the trump suit. It also has defensive potential if the opponents were to compete. You would expect to take 5 or 6 tricks if the opponents were to bid 4♠, for example. It should be opened 2♣.

With the second hand, you can take ten tricks by yourself if allowed to play in a heart contract. But you have no sure trick on defense if the opponents compete in spades or clubs. Don't open 2♣. Open 1♥ or 4♥ and try to buy the contract at a suitable level.

3. 4-4-4-1 Hands

Strong hands with 4-4-4-1 distribution are awkward to bid. Because of the singleton, you can't usually treat them as balanced, but with no five-card suit, they are difficult to treat as unbalanced. You may need to go slowly to find a fit. Look at these two hands:

a)	♠ A Q J 8	b)	♠ A K 5 3
	♥ A Q 8 4		♥ A
	♦ J		♦ A Q J 4
	♣ A K J 4		♣ A Q 8 3

Despite the 22 high-card points in the first hand, the bidding is likely to become awkward if you open 2♣ since there is no suitable rebid. Open 1♣ and hope partner responds. On the second hand, you have a similar challenge with 24 high-card points. Most players would open 2♣ anyway, treating the hand as balanced and rebidding 2NT after a 2♦ response.

4. Balanced Judgment

Be prepared to exercise some judgment with your opening bid and rebid when dealing with strong hands. Consider these two hands:

a) ♠ K Q 10   b) ♠ A K J
    ♥ A J   ♥ K 5
    ♦ A J 10 9 8   ♦ A K Q 8 7 5
    ♣ A Q 10   ♣ K 4

The first hand has 21 high-card points plus 1 length point and is worth an opening 2♣ bid. It has a five-card suit and no card lower than an eight. Describe it as a balanced hand of 22-24 points by rebidding 2NT over a 2♦ response.

The second hand should definitely be opened 2♣, with 23 high-card points plus 2 length points for the six-card suit. If partner responds 2♦, a rebid of 3♦ may leave partner awkwardly placed with a very weak hand. If partner bids 3NT, you will have to put your hand down as dummy. A heart or club opening lead may trap your king and allow the defenders to take enough tricks to defeat the contract. A more practical rebid is 3NT, treating the hand as balanced with 25-27 points. If the opening lead is a spade, a heart or a club from your left, you should easily be able to take nine tricks.

SUMMARY

Strong Opening Bids

UNBALANCED HANDS

- 22 or more   Open 2♣. This is a strong artificial forcing bid.

BALANCED HANDS

- 20–21   Open 2NT.
- 22–24   Open 2♣, planning to rebid 2NT.
- 25–27   Open 2♣, planning to rebid 3NT.

When partner opens 2♣, responder usually makes an artificial waiting response of 2♦, leaving opener room to describe the hand.

Keep the following points in mind:

- When opener shows a balanced hand, responder is not forced to bid again. Responder can use similar partnership methods to those used after a 1NT opening bid.

- When opener shows an unbalanced hand, responder is forced to bid again. With a very weak hand, responder makes a negative rebid, either the cheaper available minor suit at the three level or the cheapest bid in notrump, depending on the partnership agreement.

- If opener rebids the original major suit at the three level after responder has shown a weak hand, responder can pass. Any other rebid by opener or responder commits the partnership to the game level.

Quiz – Part I

You are the dealer with both sides vulnerable. What is your opening call with each of the following hands?

WEST	NORTH	EAST	SOUTH
			?

a) ♠ K J 8
   ♥ A Q 8 3
   ♦ K 4
   ♣ A Q J 9

b) ♠ K Q 7
   ♥ A K J
   ♦ A J 8 4
   ♣ A J 10

c) ♠ A K J 10 9 7 4
   ♥ A K J
   ♦ K Q
   ♣ 3

d) ♠ A K 8 5
   ♥ A Q
   ♦ A K Q 8
   ♣ K Q 7

e) ♠ 10 5
   ♥ A K Q 10 8 3
   ♦ A K Q 9
   ♣ 8

f) ♠ K Q 8 5
   ♥ K
   ♦ K J 6 5 2
   ♣ A K Q

g) ♠ A K 5
   ♥ K 4
   ♦ A Q J 8 7
   ♣ Q 10 5

h) ♠ A K 7 5
   ♥ A Q J 3
   ♦ 4
   ♣ A K J 4

i) ♠ K Q J 9 8 7 6
   ♥ —
   ♦ K Q J 10 4
   ♣ 7

Neither side is vulnerable and partner opens 2NT. What is your response with each of the following hands?

WEST	NORTH	EAST	SOUTH
	2NT	PASS	?

j) ♠ 9 5
   ♥ 6 2
   ♦ K Q 8 7 5
   ♣ Q J 7 3

k) ♠ Q J 8 7 3
   ♥ 4 2
   ♦ K 9 7 3
   ♣ 8 2

l) ♠ K 9 6 4
   ♥ Q 7 5 3
   ♦ Q 7 4 2
   ♣ 6

Answers to Quiz – Part I

a) **2NT**. This shows a balanced hand of 20-21 points when.

b) **2♣**. With a balanced hand and 23 high-card points, open the bidding 2♣. The hand is too strong to open 2NT.

c) **2♣**. With 21 high-card points and a strong seven-card suit, open with 2♣, planning to show a strong two-bid in spades.

d) **2♣**. This is an old-fashioned 3NT opening, showing 25-27 points. Playing weak two-bids, however, it is opened 2♣.

e) **2♣**. There are only 18 high-card points, but you can expect to take ten tricks in hearts with almost no help from partner, and the hand has defensive values.

f) **1♦**. Lots of points but they aren't working well together. This hand isn't balanced and isn't a strong two-bid in diamonds. Start slowly.

g) **2NT**. 19 high-card points plus 1 for the five-card suit make this hand worth a 2NT opening bid.

h) **1♣**. Despite all the points, you don't have a strong two-bid in any suit. If partner can't bid over 1♣, it's unlikely you have a game.

i) **1♠ (4♠)**. You can take ten tricks in your own hand but don't have a single sure trick on defense, so this hand doesn't qualify as a strong two-bid. The hand won't get passed out if you open 1♠.

j) **3NT**. Opener is showing 20-21 points and you have 8 high-card points plus 1 length point for the five-card suit. That's enough for game but not enough for slam. Nine tricks in 3NT should be easier than eleven tricks in a minor suit.

k) **3♥ (3♠)**. If the partnership uses Jacoby transfer bids, respond 3♥ to transfer opener to spades and then bid 3NT. Opener can pass with a doubleton spade and bid 4♠ with three-card or longer support. If the partnership doesn't use transfer bids, respond 3♠, asking opener to choose between 3NT and 4♠.

l) **3♣**. Use the Stayman convention to look for an eight-card major suit fit. If opener bids 3♥ or 3♠, raise to game. If opener bids 3♦, bid 3NT, despite the singleton. With no four-card major, opener likely has some length and strength in clubs.

Quiz – Part II

Your side is vulnerable. You open 2♣ and partner responds with a waiting bid of 2♦. What is your rebid with each of the following hands?

WEST	NORTH	EAST	SOUTH
			2♣
PASS	2♦	PASS	?

a) ♠ K Q 10 8
   ♥ A K Q
   ♦ J 9
   ♣ A Q J 7

b) ♠ —
   ♥ A K Q 5
   ♦ A 8 5
   ♣ A K J 9 8 3

c) ♠ A J
   ♥ K Q J 8
   ♦ A K Q 7
   ♣ A J 3

d) ♠ K Q
   ♥ A K Q J 9 7 6
   ♦ —
   ♣ A K 8 3

e) ♠ 4
   ♥ A K 5
   ♦ A K J 10 8 7 3
   ♣ A J

f) ♠ A Q
   ♥ K Q 9
   ♦ A 9 3
   ♣ A Q J 8 4

g) ♠ A K J 8 3
   ♥ A
   ♦ 3
   ♣ A K J 9 5 4

h) ♠ A K
   ♥ K 3
   ♦ A K Q 8 6 3
   ♣ K J 5

i) ♠ A K
   ♥ K Q J 4
   ♦ K Q J
   ♣ A K Q J

The opponents are vulnerable and you are not. Partner opens 2♣ and you respond with a waiting bid of 2♦. Partner rebids 2♠. What do you bid with each of the following hands?

WEST	NORTH	EAST	SOUTH
	2♣	PASS	2♦
PASS	2♠	PASS	?

j) ♠ 9 2
   ♥ 7 5
   ♦ Q 7 6 4 2
   ♣ 8 6 5 3

k) ♠ Q 9 4
   ♥ 8 2
   ♦ A 7 6 5
   ♣ 7 4 3 2

l) ♠ 4
   ♥ K 10 8 7 3
   ♦ 8 6 3
   ♣ K 9 6 3

Answers to Quiz – Part II

a) **2NT**. This shows a balanced hand with 22-24 points. Don't worry about the lack of a sure stopper in diamonds.

b) **3♣**. Your original 2♣ bid said nothing about clubs. You have to rebid 3♣ to show your suit. You plan to show hearts next.

c) **3NT**. This rebid shows a balanced hand with 25-27 points.

d) **2♥**. There's no need to jump to game with this hand. The 2♥ rebid is forcing. Leave lots of room to explore for slam.

e) **3♦**. Show your suit. Partner may become declarer in diamonds!

f) **2NT**. The hand is balanced with 22 high-card points and 1 for length.

g) **3♣**. Show the longer suit first. Later, bid and rebid the spades.

h) **3NT (3♦)**. Treat this as a strong balanced hand. If you rebid 3♦, partner may be awkwardly placed. 3NT is more likely to be successful with your hand as declarer rather than as dummy.

i) **4NT**. This shows a balanced hand of 28-30 points, is not forcing, and doesn't ask for aces.

j) **3♣ (2NT)**. You have a weak hand but opener's bid is forcing and you can't pass. If the partnership agreement is to use the cheaper minor as a second negative, rebid 3♣. Otherwise, rebid 2NT.

k) **3♠**. With support for opener's suit and enough values for the partnership to be in at least a game, raise to the three level. This leaves enough room for opener to explore for slam. A jump to 4♠ would show a weaker hand with support.

l) **3♥**. You don't have support for opener's suit but you do have too much to make a negative rebid. Bid your own suit. Opener won't expect a lot. With a good five-card suit and 8 or more points, you would make an initial positive response of 2♥.

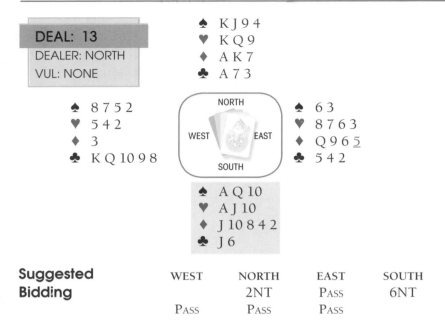

DEAL: 13
DEALER: NORTH
VUL: NONE

♠ K J 9 4
♥ K Q 9
♦ A K 7
♣ A 7 3

♠ 8 7 5 2
♥ 5 4 2
♦ 3
♣ K Q 10 9 8

NORTH
WEST   EAST
SOUTH

♠ 6 3
♥ 8 7 6 3
♦ Q 9 6 5
♣ 5 4 2

♠ A Q 10
♥ A J 10
♦ J 10 8 4 2
♣ J 6

Suggested Bidding

WEST	NORTH	EAST	SOUTH
	2NT	PASS	6NT
PASS	PASS	PASS	

With a balanced hand and 20 high-card points, North opens the bidding 2NT. When the partnership uses 2♣ as a strong artificial opening bid, an opening bid of 2NT is commonly used to show 20-21 points. With 22 or more, open 2♣ and rebid in notrump.

South has 13 high-card points plus 1 for the five-card suit. There should be enough combined strength for a small slam, but not enough for a grand slam. South should keep things simple by raising directly to 6NT. A raise to 4NT would be *quantitative*—invitational—not *Blackwood*, and North might pass with 'only' 20 points. To ask for aces directly over a notrump opening bid, 4♣, the *Gerber* convention, is used.

There's no need to ask for aces, since the partnership cannot be missing two aces with 33 or more combined high-card points. Whether the partnership has all the aces, or is missing an ace, the final contract should still be 6NT.

Suggested Opening Lead

With no indication from the auction, East will likely lead the ♦5, fourth best, or a more passive lead of the ♥8, top of nothing.

If South bids a conventional 4♣ during the auction, West might make a lead-directing double. If that happens, East would make the winning club lead for the defense.

Suggested Play

On any lead except a club, North has an easy time developing twelve tricks. There are four sure tricks in spades, three in hearts, two in diamonds, and one in clubs. Two more tricks can be developed in the diamond suit by playing the ♦A, ♦K and giving up a trick to East's ♦Q.

On a club lead, declarer is in trouble. As the cards lie, there's no way to develop more than ten tricks without giving up a trick to East's ♦Q, and the defenders can then take their club tricks.

Suggested Defense

The defenders are unlikely to find the winning club lead, unless East makes a good guess or North-South give West a chance to double clubs during the auction. If South does bid 4♣, Gerber, asking for aces, West should double, asking East to lead the suit. It's the only suit West wants led, and it's highly unlikely East will lead a club if West remains silent throughout the auction.

There's no need for North-South to give East-West any chance to exchange information during the bidding. Sometimes, a quick auction to the desired spot will bring unexpected benefits.

North's opening 2NT bid is so descriptive that South can decide HOW HIGH and WHERE in one bid and respond 6NT.

DEAL: 14
DEALER: EAST
VUL: N-S

♠ 10 8 4 2
♥ Q 10 7 4 3
♦ K 6
♣ Q 8

♠ A K J
♥ A 9 5
♦ A Q
♣ A J 6 4 3

NORTH

WEST   EAST

SOUTH

♠ Q 7 6 3
♥ 8 6 2
♦ 10 7 5
♣ K 5 2

♠ 9 5
♥ K J
♦ J 9 8 4 3 2
♣ 10 9 7

Suggested Bidding

WEST	NORTH	EAST	SOUTH
		PASS	PASS
2♣	PASS	2♦	PASS
2NT	PASS	3♣	PASS
3♦	PASS	3NT	PASS
PASS	PASS		

With 23 high-card points plus 1 length point for the five-card club suit, West is too strong for an opening bid of 2NT if the partnership range is 20–21. Instead, West starts with an artificial 2♣ opening. With only 5 points, East makes a waiting response of 2♦, waiting to hear what West has to say next. West finishes the description of the hand by rebidding 2NT, showing a balanced hand of 22–24 points.

With 5 points, East has enough to take the partnership to game. East can use the same methods as the partnership normally uses over a 2NT opening bid. This is likely to include 3♣ as the Stayman convention, asking if opener has a four-card major suit. When opener denies holding a four-card major with the 3♦ bid, East settles for game in notrump.

Suggested Opening Lead

North leads the ♥4, fourth highest from longest.

Suggested Play

Declarer can count four sure tricks in spades, one in hearts, one in diamonds, and two in clubs. One more trick is needed. This might come from a successful diamond finesse for the missing ♦K or a successful club finesse for the missing ♣Q.

One challenge is that the defenders may be able to establish enough heart tricks to defeat the contract, especially if the lead is lost to North. Declarer should start by *holding up* with the ♥A. On the third round of hearts, West must win the ♥A, but now it is only North who is the dangerous opponent. It's safe to lose a trick to South.

West should take the three top spade tricks to *unblock* the suit. Rather than staking everything on the diamond finesse, declarer should first try the extra chance that the ♣Q might be singleton or doubleton by playing the ♣A and a low club to dummy's ♣K.

On the actual hand, North's ♣Q appears on the second round, so there's no need to risk the diamond finesse. Declarer can take the ♠Q and the rest of the club winners. If the ♣Q had not fallen, West could try the diamond finesse as a second chance. If North had shown out on the second round of clubs, declarer could safely lead toward the ♣J after taking the ♠Q, rather than taking the diamond finesse. Even if both opponents had followed with low clubs, declarer would still have the option of playing a third round of clubs rather than taking the diamond finesse. As long as South has the ♣Q, North can never get the lead.

Playing the ♣A and ♣K before deciding whether to take the diamond finesse gives declarer two chances rather than one.

Suggested Defense

If South plays the ♥K on the first trick and continues with the ♥J, North should overtake with the ♥Q to continue leading the suit. Now, if declarer loses a trick to North's ♦K or ♣Q, the defense has enough tricks to defeat the contract.

The opening 2♣ bid followed by a rebid of 2NT paints a very clear picture of West's hand. After that, responder uses the Stayman convention to get to the best contract.

DEAL: 15
DEALER: SOUTH
VUL: E-W

North:
♠ K Q 7
♥ 10 7 6 4 3
♦ 8 7 4 2
♣ 9

West:
♠ 8 6 3
♥ 9 2
♦ Q J 10 6
♣ A 5 4 3

East:
♠ A 5
♥ A Q J
♦ A
♣ K Q J 10 7 6 2

South:
♠ J 10 9 4 2
♥ K 8 5
♦ K 9 5 3
♣ 8

Suggested Bidding

WEST	NORTH	EAST	SOUTH
			PASS
PASS	PASS	2♣	PASS
2♦	PASS	3♣	PASS
4♣	PASS	4NT	PASS
5♦	PASS	5NT	PASS
6♣	PASS	PASS	PASS

East has only 21 high-card points, but the seven-card suit makes this hand worth a strong two-bid. East starts with the artificial opening bid of 2♣. West makes the waiting response of 2♦. Now East rebids 3♣ to show the club suit for the first time.

With a nice hand for clubs, West raises to 4♣. At this point, East might simply jump to 6♣, hoping to find enough in the West hand to make a slam. A more scientific approach is to use the Blackwood convention, bidding 4NT to ask how many aces West holds. If West were to show no aces by responding 5♣, East could always pass and play there. Instead, West responds 5♦, showing one ace. With the partnership holding all the aces, East might now try 5NT, asking about kings and looking for a grand slam. When West responds 6♣, showing no kings, East can settle for the small slam.

Suggested Opening Lead

Holding two kings against a slam contract, it would be dangerous to lead either suit, especially knowing that East-West have all the aces. A better choice is the ♠J, top of a sequence.

Suggested Play

The spade lead establishes a spade trick for the opponents and, at first glance, it may seem that declarer has to stake everything on a successful heart finesse, but there's a much safer play.

Declarer should take advantage of dummy's excellent diamonds. Declarer can establish two additional tricks in that suit to go along with the ♦A, by driving out the ♦K. Together with the ♠A, ♥A, and seven club tricks, that's 12 tricks in all. There are two challenges, however. Declarer must avoid losing a spade trick while driving out the ♦K, and declarer will need two entries to the dummy.

After winning the ♠A, declarer should play the ♣K to draw trump and then the ♦A. Next, declarer should lead a high club—not the ♣2—and overtake with dummy's ♣A. Now the ♦Q is led. If North were to play the ♦K, declarer could ruff with a high club and play the ♣2 over to dummy to take the established diamond winners, discarding the spade loser and a heart loser.

On the actual hand, North follows with a low diamond. Now declarer should discard the spade loser. This trick loses to South's ♦K, but that's the last trick for the defense. South can lead a spade, but East ruffs with a high club and leads the carefully preserved ♣2 over to dummy. The ♥J and ♥Q are discarded on dummy's two diamond winners and declarer makes the contract without risking the heart finesse. The technique of discarding the spade loser on the losing diamond trick is referred to as discarding a *loser on a loser*.

Suggested Defense

If declarer finds the winning line, there's nothing the defense can do, but it's more likely declarer will try the heart finesse.

After the 2♣ opening, the partnership found a good 6♣ contract by using the Blackwood convention.

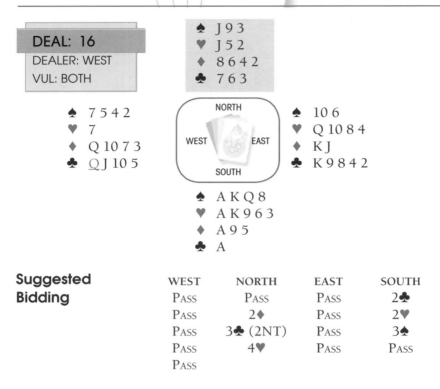

DEAL: 16
DEALER: WEST
VUL: BOTH

North hand:
- ♠ J 9 3
- ♥ J 5 2
- ♦ 8 6 4 2
- ♣ 7 6 3

West hand:
- ♠ 7 5 4 2
- ♥ 7
- ♦ Q 10 7 3
- ♣ Q J 10 5

East hand:
- ♠ 10 6
- ♥ Q 10 8 4
- ♦ K J
- ♣ K 9 8 4 2

South hand:
- ♠ A K Q 8
- ♥ A K 9 6 3
- ♦ A 9 5
- ♣ A

Suggested Bidding

WEST	NORTH	EAST	SOUTH
Pass	Pass	Pass	2♣
Pass	2♦	Pass	2♥
Pass	3♣ (2NT)	Pass	3♠
Pass	4♥	Pass	Pass
Pass			

South opens with a strong artificial 2♣ bid and North makes a 2♦ waiting response. South bids 2♥ to show a five-card or longer suit. This bid is forcing, just as if South opened with an old-fashioned strong 2♥ bid. If the partnership has agreed to use cheaper minor as second negative, North bids 3♣ to show a very weak hand. Otherwise, North rebids 2NT to show a weak hand. If South were now to rebid only 3♥, most partnerships would allow North to pass with a weak hand.

On the actual hand, South shows a second suit by bidding 3♠. With equal length in partner's suits, North gives *preference* back to 4♥. North can infer that South has more hearts than spades. With equal length, South would bid spades first. After the 4♥ bid, South has nothing more to say since North hasn't made any encouraging bids.

Suggested Opening Lead

Against 4♥, West starts with the ♣Q, top of the sequence.

Suggested Play

Declarer can afford three losers. There are two losers in diamonds, but none in spades or clubs. Declarer can afford to lose one trump trick, but not two. That will be easy if the missing hearts divide 3-2, and declarer might make an overtrick if the ♥Q falls early.

Declarer should consider what might go wrong. A problem will arise only if the missing hearts are unfavorably divided. Declarer can't do much if they are divided 5-0, but can guard against a 4-1 break.

After winning the ♣A, declarer should play the ♥A and then a low heart toward dummy. On the actual deal, West discards on the second heart and dummy's ♥J is used to force out East's ♥Q. East will likely play a club, which declarer ruffs. Knowing that East has two hearts remaining, declarer now plays the ♠8 to dummy's ♠J and leads the last heart from dummy. Declarer can finesse the ♥9 and play the ♥K to draw East's last trump. Then declarer can safely take the remaining spade winners and ♦A to make the contract.

To appreciate why declarer should lead a low heart toward dummy's ♥J after playing the ♥A, suppose the East-West hearts were exchanged with West holding ♥Q-10-8-4. Now, whether West plays the ♥Q or a low heart, declarer will get a trick with dummy's ♥J and lose only one trump trick. What if the missing hearts were divided 3-2 all along? Then, after the opponents win the second heart trick with the ♥Q, declarer still makes ten tricks after regaining the lead and drawing the last trump. Playing the ♥A and then a low heart toward the ♥J is called a *safety play* since it guarantees the contract even if the hearts are divided 4-1.

Suggested Defense

If declarer plays the ♥A-K, the unfortunate heart division gives the defenders two heart tricks to go along with their two diamond tricks. After a strong 2♣ bid, opener can take the time to describe the hand since responder is forced to keep bidding until game is reached when opener bids a new suit.

Additional
Practice Deals

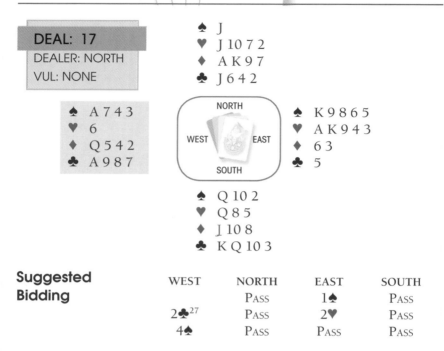

DEAL: 17
DEALER: NORTH
VUL: NONE

NORTH
♠ J
♥ J 10 7 2
♦ A K 9 7
♣ J 6 4 2

WEST
♠ A 7 4 3
♥ 6
♦ Q 5 4 2
♣ A 9 8 7

EAST
♠ K 9 8 6 5
♥ A K 9 4 3
♦ 6 3
♣ 5

SOUTH
♠ Q 10 2
♥ Q 8 5
♦ J 10 8
♣ K Q 10 3

Suggested Bidding

WEST	NORTH	EAST	SOUTH
	Pass	1♠	Pass
2♣[27]	Pass	2♥	Pass
4♠	Pass	Pass	Pass

With a borderline decision as dealer, North can apply the Guideline of 20. With 4 cards in the two longest suits—North can use any two of the three four-card suits—the total is only 18 (10 + 4 + 4). North passes. East also has a borderline opening with 10 high-card points plus 1 length point for each five-card suit. East can also apply the Guideline of 20. Adding the 10 high-card points to the number of spades and hearts, East gets a total of 20. With two five-card suits, East opens 1♠, the higher-ranking.

West has 10 high-card points and four-card support for spades. 3 dummy points can be added for the singleton heart. The total of 13 is enough to get the partnership to game. Unless the partnership has some conventional forcing raise, West can start by bidding a new suit, 2♣, planning to show the spade support at the next opportunity.

---

[27] West could make an artificial forcing raise of 2NT or a splinter response of 4♥ if the partnership uses either of these conventional bids.

North, having passed originally, might consider making a takeout double but will probably pass. East shows the second suit by bidding 2♥ and West now takes the partnership to game in spades.

Suggested Opening Lead

If West responds 2♣ to East's opening, South will probably lead the ♦J, top of the broken sequence in an unbid suit, rather than the ♣K.

Suggested Play

Unless the four missing spades are divided exactly 2-2, declarer has at least one spade loser. Declarer also has three heart losers and two diamond losers. There's nothing declarer can do about the spade and diamond losers, so declarer will have to focus on hearts. If the seven missing hearts divide 4-3, declarer can establish a heart trick through length. Declarer's plan should be to trump two heart losers in dummy, hoping to establish the last heart.

Suppose the defenders lead three rounds of diamonds and East ruffs the third round. To conserve entries, declarer can use this opportunity to play the ♥A and trump a low heart in dummy. Now declarer can draw two rounds of trumps with the ♠A and ♠K, ending in the East hand. When the missing trumps prove to be divided 3-1, declarer can leave the defender's high trump outstanding. Declarer can now take the ♥K and lead a fourth round of hearts, planning to trump in dummy.

It doesn't matter when South chooses to take the ♠Q. If South trumps the fourth round of hearts, declarer has the rest of the tricks. If South discards, declarer trumps the heart in dummy and ruffs a club or a diamond to get back to the East hand. Declarer now leads the established heart winner and South can choose when to take ♠Q. Declarer loses only two diamonds and one spade.

Suggested Defense

There is nothing the defenders can do to defeat 4♠ if declarer establishes an extra winner by ruffing two hearts in dummy.

If East didn't open, it's possible the hand would be passed out.

	♠ J 8 4

DEAL: 18
DEALER: EAST
VUL: N-S

♠ J 8 4
♥ A 9 5
♦ A K 9 6 4
♣ 6 3

♠ K 10 3
♥ K J 7 3
♦ J 7
♣ J 9 5 2

NORTH
WEST   EAST
SOUTH

♠ A 7 6 2
♥ Q 4 2
♦ Q 10 3
♣ Q 10 7

♠ Q 9 5
♥ 10 8 6
♦ 8 5 2
♣ A K 8 4

Suggested Bidding

WEST	NORTH	EAST	SOUTH
		PASS	PASS
PASS	1♦	PASS	1NT
PASS	PASS	PASS	

East, South, and West pass. After three passes, North has the option of passing the deal out. North has 12 high-card points plus 1 point for the five-card suit. That's enough to open in first, second, or third position. In fourth position, however, North can apply the Guideline of 15 to decide whether to open. 12 high-card points plus 3 spades just meets the criteria, so North opens the bidding 1♦, the long suit.

South has 9 high-card points. That's not enough to bid a new suit at the two level and South doesn't have a suit that can be bid at the one level. South responds 1NT.

North has a minimum opening. With a balanced hand, North has nothing more to say and passes. East passes, ending the auction.

Suggested Opening Lead

With a choice of four-card suits, West leads the ♥3, fourth from longest and strongest.

Suggested Play

South, declarer, has one heart trick, two diamonds, and two clubs. Two more tricks are needed. With eight diamonds in the combined hands, the best chance is to develop two extra tricks in diamonds through length. Declarer has to hope the five missing diamonds are divided 3-2 and will have to give up a diamond trick.

Declarer can hold up winning the ♥A until the third round but must then go about establishing the extra diamond winners. If declarer plays the ♦A, ♦K, and then leads a third round, dummy's remaining two diamonds will be winners when the missing diamonds prove to be divided 3-2. However, with the ♥A gone from dummy, there will be no way to get to them. Declarer must keep an entry to the long diamonds. The way to do this is to take the loss early in the diamond suit. After winning the ♥A, declarer can take one diamond winner but must then lead a low diamond and give up a trick to the defenders[28]. On regaining the lead, declarer can then get to dummy with the remaining high diamond and will be in the right place at the right time to take the two established diamond winners.

Suggested Defense

A heart lead is best for the defense, allowing the defenders to develop three heart tricks through promotion and length. When declarer gives up a diamond, the defenders can also take their two spade winners, but that's all.

North's decision to open the bidding lets the partnership get a small plus score. North-South can make 1NT or 2♦. If East and West compete to the two level, North-South can get a plus score by defending because East-West can't make any contract at the two level or higher.

---

[28] Alternatively, declarer could lose the first diamond trick.

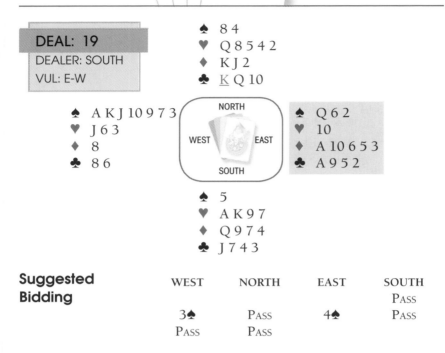

DEAL: 19 DEALER: SOUTH VUL: E-W		

NORTH
♠ 8 4
♥ Q 8 5 4 2
♦ K J 2
♣ K Q 10

WEST
♠ A K J 10 9 7 3
♥ J 6 3
♦ 8
♣ 8 6

EAST
♠ Q 6 2
♥ 10
♦ A 10 6 5 3
♣ A 9 5 2

SOUTH
♠ 5
♥ A K 9 7
♦ Q 9 7 4
♣ J 7 4 3

Suggested Bidding

WEST	NORTH	EAST	SOUTH
			PASS
3♠	PASS	4♠	PASS
PASS	PASS		

South has 10 high-card points, not enough to open even when applying the Guideline of 20 (10 + 4 + 4 = 18).

West has 9 high-card points plus 3 length points for the seven-card suit. That's not quite enough to open at the one level. With a good seven-card suit, however, West can make a preemptive opening bid. Although East and West are vulnerable, West has about seven playing tricks with spades as trumps. West can afford to overbid by two tricks. That fits with the Guideline of 500 since, if West is doubled, the penalty for being defeated two tricks is 500. West opens 3♠.

North has 11 high-card points but not enough to make a takeout double at the three level, even counting 1 dummy point for the doubleton. North's five-card heart suit isn't good enough for an overcall at the four level. North passes.

East, with the nice fit with partner's suit, has enough to raise to game. East can visualize that West will probably take seven spade tricks to go with the ♦A and ♣A, and East's singleton heart should allow West to gain a trick or two by ruffing in dummy. East has enough to raise to 4♠.

South, West, and North pass, ending the auction.

Suggested Opening Lead

North would lead the ♣K, top of the broken sequence. A lead of the ♥4, fourth highest from the long suit, would be a reasonable alternative.

Suggested Play

West, as declarer, can count three heart losers and one club loser. That's one loser too many. West's plan should be to trump at least one heart loser in dummy.

When North leads a club, declarer can actually trump two heart losers in dummy and make an overtrick. After winning the first trick with the ♣A, declarer should immediately lead a heart from dummy, giving up a trick to the defenders. Even if the defenders now lead a trump, Declarer can win in the West hand and ruff one heart loser in dummy. Declarer can then play the ♦A and ruff a diamond to get back to the West hand. Declarer's last heart can now be trumped in dummy.

Declarer loses only one heart trick and one club trick.

Suggested Defense

The defenders can't defeat the 4♠ contract, or even prevent an overtrick[29].

If West didn't open the bidding with 3♠, it's possible that the hand would get passed out. None of the other players has a clear-cut opening bid. If the hand is passed out, East-West will have missed the opportunity to make a vulnerable game.

---

[29] If North leads a trump initially to prevent declarer from ruffing two losers in dummy, declarer can use the entries to dummy to ruff diamonds three times and establish East's remaining diamond as a winner on which to discard a heart.

DEAL: 20

DEALER: WEST

VUL: BOTH

♠ A K 7 5
♥ A 8 6 3
♦ A Q
♣ A 9 4

♠ Q J 10 8
♥ Q 10
♦ J 7 6 2
♣ 7 5 2

NORTH

WEST   EAST

SOUTH

♠ 4 3
♥ K J 7 2
♦ 5 4
♣ Q J 10 8 3

♠ 9 6 2
♥ 9 5 4
♦ K 10 9 8 3
♣ K 6

Suggested Bidding

WEST	NORTH	EAST	SOUTH
PASS	2NT	PASS	3NT
PASS	PASS	PASS	

West passes.

North has a balanced hand with 21 high-card points. If the partnership uses weak two-bids and the strong artificial 2♣ opening, it typically uses a range of 20-21 points for a 2NT opening bid. This hand would then fall into the range for 2NT.

East passes.

South has 6 high-card points plus 1 length point for the five-card diamond suit. That's enough to take the partnership to a game contract of 3NT. There's no need to mention the diamond suit.

South's raise is followed by three passes, ending the auction.

Suggested Opening Lead

Against North's 3NT contract, East would lead the ♣Q, top of the solid sequence.

Suggested Play

Declarer, North, has eight sure tricks: two spades, one heart, three diamonds, and two clubs. There are several possibilities for a ninth trick. Declarer might be able to establish a spade trick through length if the six missing spades are divided 3-3. Similarly, a heart trick might be developed through length by giving up two tricks in the suit and hoping the six missing hearts are divided 3-3. However, an even number of missing cards tends to divide slightly unevenly, so the odds are against either suit dividing 3-3.

A slightly better possibility is diamonds. Declarer could win the first trick with the ♣A, play the ♦A-Q, cross to dummy's ♣K, and play the ♦K. In addition to the possibility that the six missing diamonds are divided 3-3, declarer will get all five tricks in the suit if the ♦J falls on any of the first three tricks.

But declarer doesn't need to rely on luck. The best play is to win the first trick with the ♣A, keeping the ♣K in dummy as an entry. North then takes the ♦A and plays the ♦Q, overtaking with dummy's ♦K. If the jack of diamonds doesn't fall on the first two rounds of the suit, declarer can now lead dummy's ♦10 to drive out the ♦J. That promotes dummy's remaining two diamonds as winners and the ♣K is still there as an entry.

By overtaking the ♦Q with the ♦K, declarer essentially gives up one winner, but gets two tricks in return, guaranteeing the contract. This is called a safety play.

Suggested Defense

If declarer doesn't overtake the ♦Q, the defenders are likely to defeat the contract. Even if East discards a heart, declarer can't establish an extra trick in that suit before East can establish enough club winners to defeat the contract. If declarer crosses to dummy's ♣K to take a trick with the ♦K, West's ♦J becomes a winner and declarer can't get back to dummy to take any more tricks in diamonds.

North's specific 2NT opening bid, showing a balanced hand with 20-21 points, gives enough information for South to place the contract.

	♠ 9 2
DEAL: 21	♥ J 7 3
DEALER: NORTH	♦ 10 9 7 5
VUL: NONE	♣ Q J 10 3

```
                    ♠ 9 2
                    ♥ J 7 3
                    ♦ 10 9 7 5
                    ♣ Q J 10 3
         NORTH
♠ J 7 6                      ♠ 8 5 4 3
♥ A K 9 8 5    WEST  EAST    ♥ Q 6 4
♦ 2                          ♦ A K 8 6 4
♣ A K 9 4                    ♣ 8
         SOUTH
                    ♠ A K Q 10
                    ♥ 10 2
                    ♦ Q J 3
                    ♣ 7 6 5 2
```

Suggested Bidding

WEST	NORTH	EAST	SOUTH
	PASS	PASS	1♠!
2♥	PASS	4♥?	PASS
PASS	PASS		

North passes. East doesn't have quite enough to open in second position and also passes.

South, in third position, has 12 high-card points, a borderline opening. South could apply the Guideline of 20—12 high-card points plus 8 cards in the two longest suits—but that isn't necessary in third position. Light opening bids are a reasonable tactic.

In first or second position, South would open 1♣. In third, an opening of 1♣ is less appealing. Since partner has passed, the contract may belong to East-West. If North and South do defend, South would prefer a spade lead to a club lead. A tactical opening of 1♠ is probably best. North will expect a five-card suit, but the quality of South's spades should be sufficient compensation.

After South opens 1♠, West can overcall 2♥ with the good five-card suit and 15 high-card points. North passes.

East has 9 high-card points, and with support for hearts, can count 3 dummy points for the singleton club. Opposite a two-level overcall, East has enough to take the partnership to game.

An alternative approach is for East to cuebid the opponents' suit, 2♠, showing interest in game. The auction might then go:

WEST	NORTH	EAST	SOUTH
	PASS	PASS	1♠
2♥	PASS	2♠	PASS
3♣	PASS	3♥	PASS
4♥	PASS	PASS	PASS

Suggested Opening Lead

North would lead the ♠9, top of the doubleton in partner's suit.

Suggested Play

West, declarer, has three spade losers and two club losers. There should be no heart losers if the missing hearts are divided 3-2 (but see below). Declarer's plan should be to ruff a club losers in dummy and discard a club loser on dummy's extra diamond winner.

Suggested Defense

If North leads the ♠9, South wins the first trick with the ♠Q and should then take two more spade winners. South can then continue with a fourth round of spades[30], forcing West to ruff and hoping that North can overruff.

If South does lead a fourth round of spades, the contract is defeated. If West ruffs with a low heart, North can overruff. If West ruffs with the ♥A or ♥K, North can discard. Now declarer can draw two rounds of trumps with the remaining high hearts, but North eventually gets a trick with the ♥J.

This defensive play is called an *uppercut*.

If South didn't open, or opened 1♣ instead of 1♠, North is unlikely to lead the ♠9. North will probably lead the ♣Q, top of the solid sequence. Declarer can then ruff a club, discard a club loser on the diamonds, and draw trumps to make the contract.

---

[30] It's unlikely North has the ♣A or that all declarer's clubs can be discarded on East's diamonds. North can help by discarding a low club on the third spade.

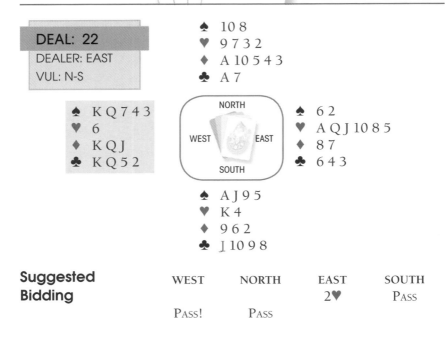

DEAL: 22
DEALER: EAST
VUL: N-S

NORTH
♠ 10 8
♥ 9 7 3 2
♦ A 10 5 4 3
♣ A 7

WEST
♠ K Q 7 4 3
♥ 6
♦ K Q J
♣ K Q 5 2

EAST
♠ 6 2
♥ A Q J 10 8 5
♦ 8 7
♣ 6 4 3

SOUTH
♠ A J 9 5
♥ K 4
♦ 9 6 2
♣ J 10 9 8

Suggested Bidding

WEST	NORTH	EAST	SOUTH
		2♥	PASS
PASS!	PASS		

East, with a good six-card suit and only 7 high-card points, has an ideal opening weak 2♥ bid. If the deal belongs to North-South, the weak two-bid will make the auction more challenging for them; if the deal belongs to East-West, the opening bid is very descriptive.

West has 16 high-card points plus 1 length point for the five-card spade suit. That's a good hand, but not opposite partner's 2♥ opening bid. West should focus on playing tricks and not high-card points. East has shown a weak hand with about five playing tricks with hearts as trumps. Without a fit for hearts, West doesn't have enough to raise to 4♥. The partnership is likely to be missing the ♠A, ♦A, and ♣A, and have at least one heart loser as well. If East does have one of the outside aces, the heart suit won't be as strong and there will likely be two or more losers in the suit. Also, there will probably not be enough tricks in a notrump contract. Even if East's hearts can be established, there is unlikely to be an entry to get to them. A response of 2♠ would be forcing and could get the partnership too high. West's best option is to pass. This will end the auction since North doesn't have enough to bid.

Suggested Opening Lead

South is on lead against 2♥. With a solid sequence in clubs, South leads the ♣J, top of the touching high cards.

Suggested Play

Declarer has a spade loser, a heart loser, a diamond loser, and two club losers. Declarer can afford five losers in a 2♥ contract.

Declarer can hope to make one or two extra tricks. If South has the ♣A, declarer could get two club tricks by leading toward the ♣K and ♣Q. After the opening lead of the ♣J, however, it's unlikely that South holds the ♣A. Declarer can also take a finesse in hearts, hoping North holds the ♥K. That won't do much good unless North has a doubleton heart since declarer can't repeat the finesse.

On the actual deal, neither of these options work. Declarer will probably be held to eight tricks…or fewer (see below)!

Suggested Defense

South's lead of the ♣J will establish two club tricks for the defense if North wins dummy's ♣Q or ♣K with the ♣A and immediately returns a club. If North returns the ♦A instead, declarer will be able to discard a club loser on dummy's extra diamond winner.

If North does return a club, the defenders could actually defeat the contract. After South wins a trick with the ♥K, South can take a club winner on which North can discard a spade. South can now play the ♠A and lead another spade for North to ruff. North can take the ♦A for the setting trick. This is a challenging defense but illustrates why East-West shouldn't get any higher after the 2♥ opening.

If West doesn't pass 2♥ and chooses to play in notrump, the defenders can establish enough tricks to defeat the contract. North can start by leading a diamond and the defenders can continue leading diamonds when they regain the lead. North can establish three diamonds to go with the defenders' two aces. North-South should get more than five tricks. Declarer can't get more than one heart trick from dummy without help from the defenders. If declarer decides to try the heart finesse, dummy won't provide even one trick!

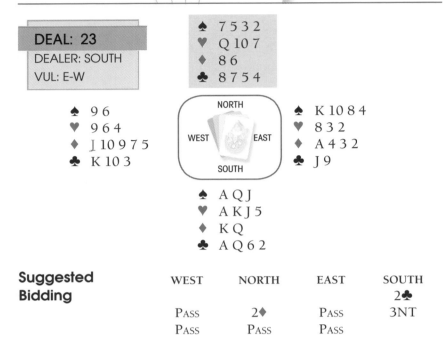

DEAL: 23
DEALER: SOUTH
VUL: E-W

♠ 7 5 3 2
♥ Q 10 7
♦ 8 6
♣ 8 7 5 4

♠ 9 6
♥ 9 6 4
♦ J 10 9 7 5
♣ K 10 3

NORTH
WEST · EAST
SOUTH

♠ K 10 8 4
♥ 8 3 2
♦ A 4 3 2
♣ J 9

♠ A Q J
♥ A K J 5
♦ K Q
♣ A Q 6 2

Suggested Bidding

WEST	NORTH	EAST	SOUTH
			2♣
PASS	2♦	PASS	3NT
PASS	PASS	PASS	

South has a balanced hand with 26 high-card points. If the partnership uses the strong artificial 2♣ opening, all hands with about 22 or more points are opened 2♣, so that is South's opening call.

After West passes, North responds with the artificial waiting bid of 2♦. This leaves South the maximum amount of bidding room to describe the hand.

East passes.

South now jumps to 3NT to show a balanced hand with 25-27 points. North has nothing more to say, so the auction ends with South as declarer in 3NT.

Suggested Opening Lead

West, on declarer's left, leads the ♦J, top of the solid sequence.

Suggested Play

After East wins the first trick with the ♦A and leads another diamond, South wins the second diamond trick and has a sure spade trick, four heart winners, and a club trick. Two more tricks are needed.

One possibility is the club suit. If East has the ♣K, a successful finesse will give declarer one extra trick, and if the missing clubs are divided 3-2, a second trick can be developed through length by giving up a club trick. The problem with this approach is that declarer can't afford to let the opponents gain the lead. The defenders are in a position to take at least four diamond tricks…more if West started with a six-card diamond suit.

A better plan is to hope that East has the ♠K. Declarer can plan to take a repeated finesse in spades. That could give declarer nine tricks without having to give up the lead. To take the repeated finesse in spades, declarer needs two entries to the North hand.

After winning the second diamond trick, declarer can lead the ♥5 over to dummy's ♥10 and then lead a low spade and finesse the ♠J. When this works, declarer can play the ♥J and overtake with dummy's ♥Q. Now declarer can repeat the finesse by playing a low spade to the ♠Q. That gives declarer nine tricks.

Suggested Defense

West's lead of the ♦J gets the defense off to a good start. East should play the ♦A on the first trick, third hand high, in case West has led from an interior sequence headed by the ♦K-J-10. When declarer's ♦Q appears on the first trick, East leads another diamond to establish West's suit. If either defender gains the lead in another suit, the defense is poised to take three more diamond tricks.

South shows a balanced hand with 25-27 points by first opening 2♣ and then rebidding 3NT. This is the partnership's best contract.

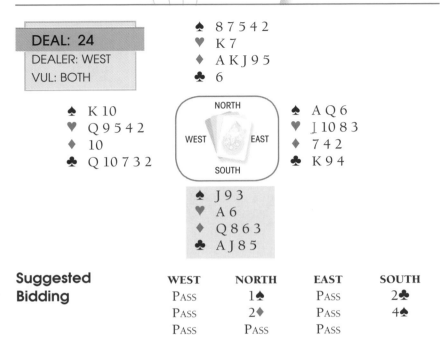

DEAL: 24
DEALER: WEST
VUL: BOTH

NORTH
♠ 8 7 5 4 2
♥ K 7
♦ A K J 9 5
♣ 6

WEST
♠ K 10
♥ Q 9 5 4 2
♦ 10
♣ Q 10 7 3 2

EAST
♠ A Q 6
♥ J 10 8 3
♦ 7 4 2
♣ K 9 4

SOUTH
♠ J 9 3
♥ A 6
♦ Q 8 6 3
♣ A J 8 5

Suggested Bidding

WEST	NORTH	EAST	SOUTH
PASS	1♠	PASS	2♣
PASS	2♦	PASS	4♠
PASS	PASS	PASS	

West has 7 high-card points plus 1 length point for each five-card suit. That isn't enough to open in first position. West passes.

North has 11 high-card points plus 1 length point for each five-card suit. That's enough to open the bidding. Although the diamonds are stronger than the spades, North bids 1♠, the higher-ranking suit. East passes.

South has 12 high-card points, and with support for partner's major suit, can add 1 dummy point for the doubleton heart. South starts by bidding a new suit. With two four-card suits, South responds up the line, bidding the cheaper, 2♣.

West passes and North shows the second suit by bidding 2♦. East passes.

South has support for diamonds as well as spades. With enough strength to go to game, South chooses the major suit, 4♠. It should be easier to take ten tricks than eleven tricks. South's jump to game is followed by three passes.

Suggested Opening Lead

East leads the ♥J, top of the broken sequence in an unbid suit.

Suggested Play

Declarer, North, has no losers in hearts, diamonds, or clubs. The only losers are in the spade suit and North can afford three losers in a contract of 4♠. So, North must hope the five missing spades are divided 3-2 and that two tricks can be developed in the suit through length.

Assuming the spades are divided 3-2, declarer's priority is to draw the missing trumps. Declarer doesn't want to lose more than three trump tricks, which might happen if one of the defenders can get a ruff. After winning the first heart trick, declarer immediately leads a spade, giving up a trick to the defenders. On regaining the lead, declarer leads another spade, giving up a second trick in the suit.

Once the missing spades prove to be divided 3-2, the contract is safe. Declarer doesn't need to draw the last trump. Instead, declarer can start taking winners, letting the defenders take their remaining trump trick whenever they wish.

Suggested Defense

The defenders can't prevent declarer from taking ten tricks if declarer draws the trumps right away. If declarer starts taking diamond winners before leading trumps, however, the contract can be defeated. West can ruff the second round of diamonds and the defenders still have three top spade winners.

By opening 1♠, even though it is a weak five-card suit, North gives enough information for South to get the partnership to the best game—even missing the A-K-Q of trumps.

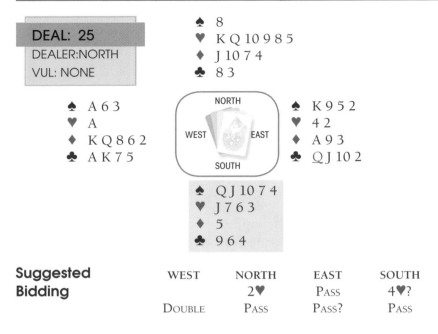

DEAL: 25
DEALER:NORTH
VUL: NONE

NORTH
♠ 8
♥ K Q 10 9 8 5
♦ J 10 7 4
♣ 8 3

WEST
♠ A 6 3
♥ A
♦ K Q 8 6 2
♣ A K 7 5

EAST
♠ K 9 5 2
♥ 4 2
♦ A 9 3
♣ Q J 10 2

SOUTH
♠ Q J 10 7 4
♥ J 7 6 3
♦ 5
♣ 9 6 4

Suggested Bidding

WEST	NORTH	EAST	SOUTH
	2♥	PASS	4♥?
DOUBLE	PASS	PASS?	PASS

North deals and has an ideal hand for an opening weak 2♥ bid—a good six-card suit and only 6 high-card points. North can expect to take at least five tricks with little help from partner. Since North-South are non-vulnerable, the penalty for being doubled and defeated three tricks is 500. So, the hand meets the Guideline of 500.

East has 10 high-card points and might count 1 dummy point for the doubleton heart when thinking about a takeout double, but that still isn't enough to enter the auction. East passes.

South has only 4 high-card points but an excellent fit with hearts. South knows the partnership has a ten-card fit and the defenders likely have enough strength for at least a game, if not a slam. South's best tactic is to take further preemptive action by jumping to 4♥.

West is faced with a challenge when North-South have bid 4♥ before West has an opportunity to start describing the hand. With 20 high-card points plus 1 point for the five-card suit, West's most flexible action is to double. Although North-South are in game, West's double isn't purely penalty. West can't be expected to hold much in hearts in this auction, so the double is based on high-card strength.

After North passes, therefore, East may decide to bid rather than pass. 4♥ is likely to be defeated at least a couple of tricks, but that may not be sufficient compensation for a possible East-West game or slam. The challenge, however, is to decide which suit and how high to bid. East can expect support for the unbid suits from West, but there's no guarantee it will be enough. With no clear-cut choice, East may pass and accept the "sure" plus score for defeating 4♥.

Suggested Opening Lead

If North is left as declarer in 4♥ doubled, East might choose the ♣Q, top of the solid sequence. A trump lead would also be a good choice. Since East and West probably have most of the high cards, they want to prevent declarer from ruffing their winners.

Suggested Play

Declarer, North, has a spade loser, a heart loser, four diamond losers, and two club losers. That's a lot of losers, but North-South aren't expecting to make 4♥. Declarer's plan should be to ruff at least two diamond losers in dummy. On gaining the lead, declarer should immediately lead a diamond. If the defenders don't lead hearts quickly enough, declarer may be able to ruff three diamonds in dummy.

At worst, declarer will lose a spade, a heart, two diamonds, and two clubs. That's two down and a penalty of 300 points, doubled and non-vulnerable. If declarer gets to ruff three diamonds, the contract is defeated only one trick for a penalty of 100 points.

Suggested Defense

The defenders should try to lead two rounds of trumps to prevent declarer from ruffing three diamond losers. If East wins the first trick with the ♣Q, for example, East can lead a heart to West's ♥A. East can then win a trick with the ♦A to lead a second heart.

A penalty of 100 or 300 points isn't much compensation for East-West. They can make game in notrump, diamonds, and even spades. They can also make a slam with clubs as trumps.

DEAL: 26

DEALER: EAST

VUL: N-S

♠ A 8
♥ 9 7 4
♦ 10 9 5
♣ K J 9 5 3

♠ K Q J 7
♥ K J 6 5
♦ A K J
♣ A 6

NORTH
WEST   EAST
SOUTH

♠ 10 4 2
♥ Q 10 3 2
♦ Q 7 4 3
♣ 8 4

♠ 9 6 5 3
♥ A 8
♦ 8 6 2
♣ Q 10 7 2

Suggested Bidding

WEST	NORTH	EAST	SOUTH
		PASS	PASS
2♣	PASS	2♦	PASS
2NT	PASS	3♣	PASS
3♥	PASS	4♥	PASS
PASS	PASS		

East and South pass. West has a balanced hand and 22 high-card points. This is too strong for an opening 2NT if the partnership range is 20-21. Instead, West starts with 2♣. North passes.

East has 4 high-card points and makes the artificial waiting response of 2♦. South passes. West describes a balanced hand of 22-24 points by rebidding 2NT.

North passes and East has enough to take the partnership to game. With a four-card heart suit, East looks for an eight-card major suit fit by using the Stayman convention. East bids 3♣.

West has four cards in both majors. A standard agreement is to bid "up the line."[31]

North passes and East raises to game in hearts by bidding 4♥. East's bid is followed by three passes, ending the auction.

---

[31] Technically it doesn't matter which suit West bids first.

Suggested Opening Lead

Against a suit contract, a lead of the top of touching high cards is often safer than leading away from an honor, so North might lead the ♦10. North might also choose to lead the ♠A hoping to get a ruff in the suit, a low club hoping to establish winners in that suit, or the passive lead of a trump. Sometimes, there's no clear choice.

Suggested Play

Declarer, West, has a spade loser, a heart loser, and a club loser. West can afford three losers, so the contract is in no danger unless the defenders can get a ruff. On gaining the lead, declarer's priority is to draw the outstanding trumps. West can use one of the heart honors to drive out the defenders' ♥A and then draw the remaining trumps on regaining the lead. Then declarer can promote three winners in the spade suit by driving out the ♠A.

If North leads a diamond initially, declarer can make an overtrick. After winning the first diamond, declarer drives out the ♥A and draws the remaining trumps after regaining the lead. Declarer can then discard the club loser on dummy's extra diamond winner.

Suggested Defense

The defenders can't defeat 4♥. North's lead, will only determine whether declarer makes an overtrick. If North finds a club lead, the defense can get three tricks … the ♥A, the ♠A, and a club.

North can also hold declarer to ten tricks by leading the ♠A and continuing with a second spade. On gaining the lead with the ♥A, South can lead a third round of spades for North to ruff. However, that's the last trick for the defense. Declarer can draw the remaining trumps and discard the club loser.

If East-West don't use the Stayman convention and reach 3NT, the contract can be defeated. A club lead by either defender will establish four club winners for the defense. Together with the ♠A and ♥A, the contract can be defeated two tricks.

DEAL: 27		♠ 6
DEALER: SOUTH		♥ K Q 9 7 4 3
VUL: E-W		◆ J 6
		♣ J 7 6 2

	NORTH	
♠ J 9 7 3		♠ Q 8 4
♥ 10 2	WEST EAST	♥ A J 8 6
◆ K 8 3		◆ 5 2
♣ K Q 10 3	SOUTH	♣ A 9 8 5

♠ A K 10 5 2
♥ 5
◆ A Q 10 9 7 4
♣ 4

Suggested Bidding

WEST	NORTH	EAST	SOUTH
			1◆
PASS	1♥	PASS	1♠
PASS	2♥	PASS	2♠
PASS	3◆	PASS	PASS
PASS			

To describe 6-5 distribution, the standard approach is to open the six-card suit, planning to bid and rebid the five-card suit. So, South starts with 1◆. West and East pass throughout the auction.

North responds 1♥. South introduces the second suit by bidding 1♠. At this point, North is unaware that South has a very distributional hand. South might bid the same way with four diamonds and four spades. With no fit with either suit, North will probably choose to rebid 2♥.

Now South finishes the description by rebidding 2♠. By bidding spades twice, South is showing a five-card suit. By inference, South must also hold at least six diamonds. With five spades and five diamonds, South would start with the higher-ranking suit, 1♠. Opposite such an unbalanced hand, a notrump contract is unlikely to fare well. North should give preference back to 3◆, putting the partnership in its eight-card fit. Passing 2♠ would leave the partnership a level lower but in a six-card fit—which could be disastrous if the trump suit breaks badly. Having fully described the hand and receiving no encouragement from partner, South settles for partscore.

Suggested Opening Lead

West will probably lead the ♣K, top of the touching honors from the broken sequence in the unbid suit. Alternatively, West might visualize from the auction that declarer may have some spade losers to trump in the dummy. To minimize this, West might lead a low diamond.

Suggested Play

Whether or not the defenders lead a trump, declarer will have the opportunity to ruff at least one spade loser in dummy. Declarer can also plan to establish a winner through length in the spade suit. Since the missing spades divide 4-2, declarer's fifth spade will eventually be established as a winner.

If the defenders never lead diamonds, declarer can ruff two spade losers in dummy and finish with an overtrick. After the trumps are drawn, declarer's remaining spade will be a winner.

Suggested Defense

The defense should try to prevent declarer from ruffing spade losers in the dummy. If West leads the ♣K, the best defense is for East to overtake with the ♣A and lead a diamond. If declarer tries the diamond finesse, West can win the ♦K and lead a second round of diamonds to remove dummy's last trump. Declarer will eventually lose two spades, a heart, a diamond, and a club [32].

If South plays in 2♠, West should lead the ♣K, hoping to force declarer to ruff. Since West holds four spades, the defenders will then have as many trumps as declarer. This will make the play uncomfortable for declarer and the defense may defeat a 2♠ contract.

By opening the longer suit first, South helps North determine the best trump suit for the partnership.

---

[32] Declarer can still make 3♦ if East leads a diamond. Declarer has to win the ♦A instead of trying the finesse. Declarer can then ruff one spade loser in dummy.

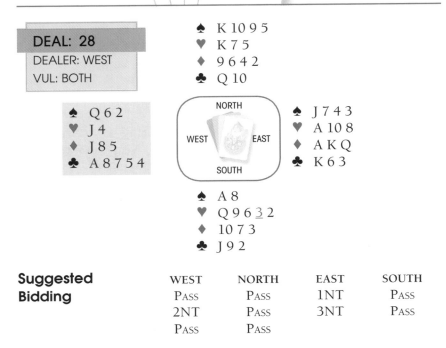

DEAL: 28
DEALER: WEST
VUL: BOTH

NORTH
♠ K 10 9 5
♥ K 7 5
♦ 9 6 4 2
♣ Q 10

WEST
♠ Q 6 2
♥ J 4
♦ J 8 5
♣ A 8 7 5 4

EAST
♠ J 7 4 3
♥ A 10 8
♦ A K Q
♣ K 6 3

SOUTH
♠ A 8
♥ Q 9 6 3 2
♦ 10 7 3
♣ J 9 2

Suggested Bidding

WEST	NORTH	EAST	SOUTH
PASS	PASS	1NT	PASS
2NT	PASS	3NT	PASS
PASS	PASS		

West and North don't have enough to open the bidding, so the auction will begin with two passes.

East has 17 high-card points and a balanced hand. East opens the bidding 1NT. South passes.

West has 8 high-card points and can add 1 length point for the five-card club suit. That's enough to invite the partnership to game by raising to 2NT. West doesn't have to be concerned that East has opened light in third position. A 1NT opening shows 15-17 in any position at the table.

With a maximum, 17 points, East accepts the invitation and bids 3NT. This is followed by three passes and East becomes declarer in 3NT.

Suggested Opening Lead

South leads the ♥3, fourth highest from the longest suit.

Suggested Play

East, declarer, has one sure heart trick, three diamonds, and two clubs. Three more tricks are required. After the heart lead, East can get a second trick in hearts by playing the ♥4 from dummy.. If North were to play a low heart on the first trick, East could win the ♥10 and still have the ♥A. On the actual deal, North will play the ♥K, third hand high. East wins the ♥A, and the ♥J-10 can be used to promote another trick by driving out the ♥Q. Of course, East won't do that right away. There are other priorities... and North-South will likely be the side leading hearts later in the play.

To get the other two tricks needed for the contract, declarer should plan to develop two tricks through length in the club suit. Only five clubs are missing and, hopefully, they will be divided 3-2. Declarer can win two tricks with the ♣A-K and give up one trick to the defenders, establishing dummy's remaining two clubs as winners. The challenge is that the ♣A is the only sure entry to the dummy, so declarer must be sure to apply the guideline of "take the losses early."

After winning the ♥A, declarer should take the ♣K and lead a second club, playing low from dummy, giving a trick to the defenders[33]. The defenders win this trick and will likely continue leading hearts to establish South's suit. When they do this, declarer will get a second heart trick. Declarer can now take the ♣A and is in the right place at the right time to take the two established club winners in dummy.

Declarer finishes with two heart tricks, three diamonds, and four clubs. That's enough tricks to make 3NT.

Suggested Defense

The defenders can't prevent declarer from taking nine tricks on this deal.

Although the strength requirement for one of a suit can vary from position to position around the table, the strength for a 1NT opening remains the same.

---

[33] Alternatively, declarer could play a low club from both hands on the first round of clubs.

DEAL: 29
DEALER: NORTH
VUL: NONE

♠ Q 10 8 4 2
♥ 4
♦ K 8 5 2
♣ 9 7 4

♠ 9 7 6
♥ J 9 6 3
♦ Q 4
♣ A 10 6 3

NORTH
WEST EAST
SOUTH

♠ A K
♥ A K Q 10 8 7
♦ A 6
♣ K J 5

♠ J 5 3
♥ 5 2
♦ J 10 9 7 3
♣ Q 8 2

Suggested Bidding

WEST	NORTH	EAST	SOUTH
	PASS	2♣	PASS
2♦	PASS	2♥	PASS
3♥	PASS	4NT	PASS
5♦	PASS	5NT	PASS
6♣	PASS	6♥	PASS
PASS	PASS		

North passes. East has 24 high-card points plus 2 length points for the six-card heart suit. East starts the bidding with a strong artificial 2♣. West makes the waiting response of 2♦[34].

East shows an unbalanced hand with a five-card or longer suit by rebidding 2♥. This is a forcing bid since East's strength is unlimited. West shows the heart fit by raising to 3♥. Once a trump suit has been agreed, the partnership is committed to at least game, so West doesn't need to jump. The partnership wants to leave room to explore a possible slam.

East has enough extra strength to consider a slam. The straightforward approach is to use the Blackwood convention, 4NT, to ask for aces.

[34] In some partnerships, West might make a positive response of 2NT with this hand. East would then rebid 3♥, West would raise to 4♥, and the auction would continue as above.

West's 5♦ reply shows one ace and East can now contemplate a grand slam if West has the missing king. East's 5NT bid asks about kings and West's 6♣ bid shows none. East settles for 6♥.

Suggested Opening Lead

South leads the ♦J, top of the solid three-card sequence.

Suggested Play

Declarer, East, will probably try to win the first trick with dummy's ♦Q, but North will cover with the ♦K. Declarer wins the ♦A and has a diamond loser and a club loser. One possibility of eliminating a loser is to guess which defender holds the ♣Q. However, declarer can guarantee the contract with the help of an *end play*.

After winning the ♦A, declarer draws trumps in two rounds. Then declarer takes the ♠A and ♠K. Next, declarer goes to dummy with a heart winner and leads dummy's last spade and trumps it. That eliminates the spades in the East-West hands. Finally, declarer gives the defenders their diamond trick by leading a diamond. That eliminates the diamonds from the East-West hands.

Whichever defender wins the diamond trick has no winning option. If the defender leads a club, declarer is assured of three club tricks. If the defender leads a spade or a diamond, declarer gets a *ruff and a sluff*–declarer can ruff in dummy and discard (sluff) the club loser from declarer's hand.

The key to an end play is to eliminate all the defenders' favorable options before putting them on lead. On this deal, declarer eliminates the defenders' trumps and then the spades and diamonds in the East-West hands so that the defenders can't effectively lead either of those suits. At the end, the defenders are forced to lead a club, eliminating declarer's guess in that suit.

Suggested Defense

The Diamond lead gets the defenders off to the best start but the contract can't be defeated if declarer avoids losing a club trick.

The 2♣ opening bid provides a lot of room to explore slam possibilities once the trump suit has been established.

```
DEAL: 30
DEALER: EAST
VUL: N-S
```

North:
- ♠ J 9
- ♥ Q 6 4
- ♦ Q 9
- ♣ Q J 10 7 5 2

West:
- ♠ 8 5 4 2
- ♥ A J
- ♦ A 10 8 4 2
- ♣ A 8

East:
- ♠ A K 7 3
- ♥ K 8 5 2
- ♦ 7 6 5
- ♣ K 4

South:
- ♠ Q 10 6
- ♥ 10 9 7 3
- ♦ K J 3
- ♣ 9 6 3

Suggested Bidding

WEST	NORTH	EAST	SOUTH
		1♦	PASS
1♠	PASS	2♠	PASS
4♠[35]	PASS	PASS	PASS

East is the dealer and has 13 high-card points, enough to open the bidding. With no five-card major suit, East opens the longer minor suit, 1♦.

South passes. West has 13 high-card points plus 1 length point for the five-card diamond suit, enough to take the partnership to game opposite East's opening bid. Although West has excellent support for diamonds, the first priority is to look for a major-suit fit. An eight-card major-suit fit is preferable to a fit in a minor suit. West responds 1♠, despite the meager holding.

North is not strong enough to make a two-level overcall in clubs and passes.

East has four-card support for responder's spades and, with a minimum opening, raises to the cheapest level 2♠.

---

[35] West might take a different route to game. Most partnerships would treat 3♦ as forcing after spades have been raised. Alternatively, West might jump to 3NT, but East should go back to 4♠.

After South passes, West has enough strength to take the partnership to game. West finishes as declarer in a 4♠ contract.

Suggested Opening Lead

North leads the ♣Q, top of the solid three-card sequence.

Suggested Play

West, the declarer, counts the losers. There are no losers in hearts or clubs. In spades, there will only be one loser if the five missing trumps divide 3-2. Also, there will be two diamond losers if the missing diamonds are divided 3-2. Declarer's plan is to establish both the spades and diamonds through length.

After winning the first club trick, declarer draws two rounds of trumps with the ♠A-K and then leaves the defenders' high trump outstanding. Next, declarer plays the ♦A and gives up a diamond trick. The defenders can win and take their spade winner but will then have to give the lead back to declarer. West gives up one more diamond trick to the opponents and then has all the remaining tricks, since the diamonds are now established.

Suggested Defense

There is nothing the defenders can do to defeat the contract if declarer establishes the diamonds before taking the remaining winners in hearts and clubs.

4♠ is the only game contract East-West can make. If East-West get to 5♦, there are two diamond losers and a spade loser. Finding an eight-card major suit fit is a priority after an opening bid of 1♣ or 1♦.

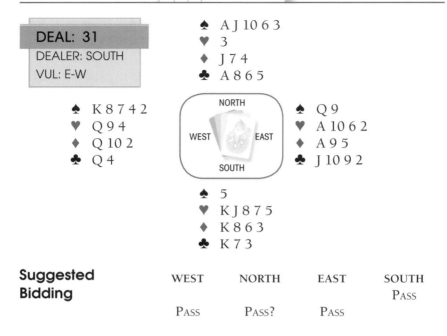

DEAL: 31

DEALER: SOUTH
VUL: E-W

North hand:
- ♠ A J 10 6 3
- ♥ 3
- ♦ J 7 4
- ♣ A 8 6 5

West hand:
- ♠ K 8 7 4 2
- ♥ Q 9 4
- ♦ Q 10 2
- ♣ Q 4

East hand:
- ♠ Q 9
- ♥ A 10 6 2
- ♦ A 9 5
- ♣ J 10 9 2

South hand:
- ♠ 5
- ♥ K J 8 7 5
- ♦ K 8 6 3
- ♣ K 7 3

Suggested Bidding

WEST	NORTH	EAST	SOUTH
			PASS
PASS	PASS?	PASS	

None of the players has a real opening bid, so the deal should get passed out. That may not happen, however.

South has 10 high-card points plus 1 length point for the five-card suit. Even using the Guideline of 20, there isn't quite enough to open in first position... 10 high-card points plus 5 hearts plus 4 diamonds = 19. Similarly, West has only 9 high-card points plus 1 length point for the five-card suit.

North has 10 high-card points plus 1 for the five-card suit. That's not a full opening bid, but North might consider opening light in third position. That's often a good tactic, but North needs to be prepared for what might happen next. It will be fine if South raises spades. Also, a new suit response isn't forcing once partner passed originally, so North can pass if South responds 2♣ or 2♦. If South responds 2♥, however, North will be awkwardly placed. Passing is likely to leave the partnership in a poor contract but bidding again may get the partnership too high. Opening 1♠ with this hand, therefore, is a risky venture. The safer course is to pass.

East has 11 high-card points. With a borderline hand in fourth position, East can use the Guideline of 15. 11 high-card points plus 2 spades is only a total of 13, so East should pass.

Suggested Opening Lead, Play, and Defense

The deal is likely to be passed out.

If North does open 1♠, the auction is likely to get uncomfortable. South has enough to respond 2♥ and the partnership will already be overboard no matter what North does next.

This deal is included to show that there are risks to opening light in third position. It's a good idea with the right type of hand, but it doesn't come with any guarantee!

DEAL: 32
DEALER: WEST
VUL: BOTH

♠ A 6
♥ J 3
♦ K Q 10 9 8 6
♣ 8 7 3

♠ Q J 10 7 4
♥ Q 8 5
♦ 5
♣ K 10 6 2

NORTH
WEST   EAST
SOUTH

♠ 9 8 2
♥ K 9 7 4
♦ J 7 4 2
♣ J 9

♠ K 5 3
♥ A 10 6 2
♦ A 3
♣ A Q 5 4

Suggested Bidding

WEST	NORTH	EAST	SOUTH
Pass	2♦	Pass	2NT
Pass	3♠	Pass	3NT
Pass	Pass	Pass	

West is the dealer and doesn't have enough to open the bidding.

North has a good six-card suit but only 10 high-card points. North's hand is suitable for a weak 2♦ opening. Even though North and South are vulnerable, the 2♦ opening is descriptive and not too risky. North can expect to take about five diamond tricks and a spade trick, a total of six tricks. That's two down if doubled and vulnerable, which fits in with the Guideline of 500.

East passes. South has a balanced hand with 17 high-card points and a fit with North's diamonds. Since the weak two-bid can be made on as few as 5 high-card points, however, South can use the artificial 2NT response to ask for a further description of North's hand[36].

West passes.

With the upper range for the weak two-bid, North can bid 3♠, showing an outside feature.

---

[36] South might simply jump to 3NT, expecting to take six diamond tricks, two aces, and perhaps a trick with the ♠K or ♣Q.

East passes and South has sufficient information to know that 3NT should be a reasonable contract. Even if the diamond suit isn't solid, North will have a side entry in the spade suit. South's 3NT call is followed by three passes, ending the auction.

Suggested Opening Lead

West leads the ♠Q, top of the solid sequence.

Suggested Play

Declarer, South, has two spade tricks, one heart, three diamonds, and one club. Two more tricks are required. The diamond suit should provide the extra tricks through length or promotion. In case the missing diamonds aren't divided 3-2, declarer wants to keep an entry on the same side of the table as the long suit.

To keep dummy's ♠A as an entry, declarer wins the first trick with the ♠K. Declarer takes a trick with the ♦A and then leads the ♦3 toward dummy. When West discards, declarer wins dummy's ♦K and ♦Q and continues with another diamond to drive out East's ♦J. Declarer still has the ♠A as an entry to dummy's established diamond winners after regaining the lead.

Declarer wins two spades, one heart, five diamonds, and a club. That's nine tricks.

Suggested Defense

The defenders can't defeat the contract provided declarer retains dummy's ♠A as an entry to dummy.

An opening weak two-bid is both obstructive and constructive. Responder is well placed to decide WHERE and HOW HIGH the partnership belongs.

Glossary

Artificial Bid—A call during the auction which, by partnership agreement, carries a special message unrelated to the suit bid. For example, 2♣, a strong opening bid, doesn't necessarily show clubs. (page 95)

Balanced Hand—A hand with no voids, no singletons, and at most one doubleton. There are only three balanced hand patterns: 4–3–3–3; 4–4–3–2, and 5–3–3–2. See also semi-balanced hand. (page 2)

Balance (Balancing)—Bidding when a pass would mean the opponents could buy the contract at a low level. 1♥—Pass—Pass to you. (page 26)

Better Minor—Opening the bidding in the longer minor suit, or the stronger of two equal-length minor suits, when there is no five-card or longer major suit in the hand. (page 9)

Bid—An undertaking to win at least a specified number of tricks in a specified strain: clubs, diamonds, hearts, spades, or notrump. (page 1)

Blackwood Convention—An artificial bid of 4NT after a trump suit has been agreed upon, asking for the number of aces held by partner. A response of 5♣ shows 0 aces or all 4; 5♦ shows 1 ace; 5♥ shows 2 aces; 5♠ shows 3 aces. A subsequent bid of 5NT asks for the number of kings held by partner. (page 114)

Broken Sequence—A sequence of cards in a suit where the third card from the top is missing but not the next lower-ranking card(s). For example, ♥K-Q-10-9, ♦J-10-8. (page 92)

Call—Any bid, double, redouble, or pass. (page 3)

Cheaper Minor Second Negative—After an opening bid of 2♥, 2♠, or 3♣ by opener and a 2♦ waiting response, an agreement that a bid of the cheaper minor suit shows a very weak hand. If opener bids 3♦, 3NT is used by responder to show a weak hand. (page 99)

Constructive Bid—A bid that suggests strength but is not forcing. An opening bid at the one-level is constructive. (page 61)

Decider—A term applied to the partner who is in a position to determine How High and Where the partnership belongs. (page 2)

Defensive Values—High cards that are likely to take tricks if the opponents win the auction and your side defends. (page 62)

Describer—A term typically applied to opener, who gives a picture of the strength and shape of the hand to responder. (page 2)

Distribution—The number of cards held in each suit by a particular player; or the number of cards held in a particular suit by the partnership; or the manner in which a suit is divided among all four hands. (page 1)

Double—A call that increases the bonus for making or defeating a contract. It can also be used to ask partner to bid a suit. (page 28)

Doubleton—A holding of two cards in a suit. A "worthless" doubleton has no high cards. (page 2)

Drury—An artificial 2♣ response to an opening bid of 1♥ or 1♠ in third or fourth position asking whether opener has a light opening bid. In standard Drury, a rebid of 2♦ by opener shows a light opening bid; in reverse Drury, a rebid of the major shows a light opening bid. (page 45)

Dummy Points—Points used in place of length points when valuing a hand in support of partner's suit: void, 5 points; singleton, 3 points; doubleton, 1 point. (page 13)

End Play—The technique of forcing an opponent to make a favorable lead during the play. It typically occurs near the end of the deal when other options have been removed from the opponents' hands. (page 149)

Equal Vulnerability—When both sides are non-vulnerable or both sides are vulnerable. (page 39)

Favorable Vulnerability—When your side is non-vulnerable and the opponents are vulnerable. (page 39)

Five-Card Majors—The partnership agreement that an opening bid of 1♥ or 1♠ promises five or more cards in the suit. (page 8)

First Position/Chair/Seat—The dealer, who is the first player to have the chance to bid or pass. (page 2)

Forcing (Bid)—A bid partner is not expected to pass. (page 33)

Fourth Highest—A lead of the fourth card down from the top in a suit. (page 24)

Fourth Position/Chair/Seat—The player to the dealer's right. The fourth player to have the chance to make a call. (page 33)

Frozen Suit—A suit in which the first side to lead the suit sacrifices a trick. (page 93)

Gambling 3NT—An opening bid of 3NT based on the playing tricks from a long solid suit rather than high-card points. (page 101)

Gerber Convention—An artificial bid of 4♣ over a bid of 1NT or 2NT asking for the number of aces held by partner. A response of 4♦ shows 0 aces or all 4; 4♥ shows 1 ace; 4♠ shows 2 aces; 4NT shows 3 aces. A subsequent bid of 5♣ asks for the number of kings held by partner. (page 114)

Guideline (Rule) of 15—In borderline cases in fourth position, high-card points are added to the number of spades in the hand. If the total is 15 or more, the suggestion is to open the bidding. Otherwise, pass. (page 36)

Guideline (Rule) of 20—In borderline cases in first or second position, the high-card points are added to the number of cards in the two longest suits. If the total is 20 or more, consider opening the bidding; otherwise pass. (page 2)

Guideline (Rule) of 500—Overbidding by two tricks when vulnerable and three tricks when non vulnerable to avoid going down more than 500 points even if doubled. Also known as the *Guideline (Rule) of Two and Three*. (page 64)

Guideline (Rule) of One, Two, and Three—Overbidding by one trick at unfavorable vulnerability, two tricks at equal vulnerability, and three tricks at favorable vulnerability when making a preemptive opening bid. (page 78)

Guideline of Two and Three—See *Rule of 500*. (page 64)

Guideline (Rule) of Two, Three, and Four—Overbidding by two tricks at unfavorable vulnerability, three tricks at equal vulnerability, and four tricks at favorable vulnerability when making a preemptive opening bid. (page 79)

High Cards—The top four cards in each suit: ace, king, queen, and jack. (page 1)

High Card Points (HCPs)—The value of high cards in a hand: ace, 4; king, 3; queen, 2; jack, 1. (page 1)

Hold Up—Letting the opponents win a trick that you could win. (page 55)

How High—The level at which the contract should be played. (page 4)

Invitational Bid—A bid which encourages partner to continue bidding but allows partner to pass with minimum values. (page 5)

Jacoby Transfer Bid—An artificial response to a 1NT opening bid where 2♦ asks opener to bid 2♥ and 2♥ asks opener to bid 2♠. Transfer bids can also be used over other notrump opening bids. (page 6)

Jacoby 2NT—An artificial response of 2NT to an opening bid of 1♥ or 1♠ that shows support for opener's suit and at least enough strength for the partnership to get to game. (page 41)

Law of Total Tricks—A statistical observation that leads to a guideline for competitive auctions that a partnership should generally compete to the level corresponding to the number of combined trumps held by the partnership. For example, with 9 combined trumps, compete to the three level—9 tricks. (page 69)

Length Points—The valuation assigned to long suits in a hand: five-card suit, 1 point; six-card suit, 2 points; seven-card suit, 3 points; eight-card suit, 4 points. (page 1)

Light (Opening)—An opening bid with less strength than would typically be expected. (page 34)

Limit Raise—An invitational jump raise of opener's suit to the three level, showing about 11-12 points. (page 13)

Loser on a Loser—Discarding a card that must be lost on a losing trick in another suit. This technique can be useful in many situations. (page 119)

Major (Suit)—Hearts or spades. (page 8)

Minor (Suit)—Clubs or diamonds. (page 9)

MUD (Middle Up Down)—A partnership agreement to lead the middle (M) card from a holding of three low cards. The highest card (Up) is played on the second round of the suit, followed by the lowest (Down) card. (page 91)

Non-Vulnerable—A side, in rubber bridge, that has not won a game. In duplicate bridge, the vulnerability is assigned. The penalties for undertricks and the bonuses for games and slams are less than when vulnerable. (page 39)

Obstructive Bid—A bid intended to interrupt the opponents' bidding conversation. A preempt. (page 61)

Offensive Value—High cards and long suits that are likely to take tricks if your side wins the auction. (page 62)

Pearson Points—See *Guideline of 15*. (page 36)

Penalty Double—A double made with the intention of increasing the bonus for defeating the opponents' contract. (page 86)

Playing Tricks—The tricks expected to be won from a hand when the contract is played in a specified strain. (page 61)

Positive Response (to 2♣ Opening)—A response to an opening bid of 2♣ that shows about 8 or more points. (page 97)

Preemptive Opening Bid—An opening bid in a suit at the two level or higher, showing a long suit and a weak hand. (page 61)

Preference—Returning to the first suit that partner bid is called giving preference. (page 120)

Quantitative—A natural, non-forcing bid that limits the strength of the hand to a narrow range. After a 1NT opening, a response of 2NT is quantitative showing 8 or 9 points. Opener could pass or bid on. (page 114)

Rebid—A player's second or subsequent bid. (page 4)

Reverse (by Opener)—A rebid by opener in a new suit that prevents responder from returning to opener's original suit at the two level. (page 14)

Reverse Drury—See Drury. (page 45)

Ruff and Sluff—A situation in a trump contract when both partnership hands have at least one trump and are void in a suit led by the opponents. The suit can be ruffed (trumped) in one hand while a loser can be sluffed (discarded) from the other hand. (page 149)

Rule—A term that is often used when 'guideline' is meant. For example, the *Rule of 20*. (page 2)

Rule of 15—See *Guideline of 15*. (page 36)

Rule of 20—See *Guideline of 20*. (page 2)

Rule of 500—See *Guideline of 500*. (page 64)

Rule of One, Two, and Three —See *Guideline of One, Two, and Three*. (page 79)

Rule of Two and Three—See *Guideline of 500*. (page 79)

Rule of Two, Three, and Four —See *Guideline of Two, Three, and Four*. (page 79)

Safety Play—The potential sacrifice of one or more overtricks to improve the chance of making a contract. (page 121)

Second Position/Chair/Seat—The player to the left of the dealer. The second person to make a call in the auction. (page 2)

Semi-balanced hand—A hand that might be suitable for a notrump contract even though it has more than one doubleton: 5-4-2-2 or 6-3-2-2 distribution. (page 15)

Short Club—An opening bid of 1♣ with fewer than four cards in the suit. Frequently used when the hand has no five-card or longer major suit. (page 9)

Singleton—A holding of one card in a suit. (page 2)

Solid Sequence—Three or more consecutive cards in a suit, headed by an honor. (page 24)

Stayman Convention—An artificial response of 2♣ to an opening bid of 1NT, asking if opener has a four-card or longer major suit. Stayman can also be used over other notrump opening bids. (page 6)

Strength—The point count value of a hand: high-card points plus distributional points. (page 1)

Strong Two-Bid—An opening bid in a suit at the two level that is forcing to the game level. (page 95)

Third Position/Chair/Seat—The partner of the dealer. The person making the third call in the auction. (page 33)

Top of Nothing— A partnership agreement to lead the top card from a holding of three low cards. (page 91)

Trick-taking Potential—The number of tricks that a hand can be expected to take. (page 1)

Two Notrump Response to a Weak Two-Bid—An artificial response to a weak two-bid, asking about opener's strength. With a minimum, opener rebids the suit at the three level; with a maximum, opener bids a new suit that shows a feature (ace or king) or bids 3NT with no feature. (page 74)

Unbalanced Hand—A hand with a void, a singleton, or more than one doubleton. (page 1)

Unblock—Play or discard high cards in a suit from one hand to gain advantage in the opposite hand. (page 117)

Unfavorable Vulnerability—When your side is vulnerable and the opponents are non-vulnerable. (page 40)

Uppercut—A defensive play which promotes a trump card into a winning trick. (page 133)

Void—A holding of zero cards in a suit. (page 2)

Vulnerability—The status of the hand during a round of bridge which affects the size of the bonuses awarded for making or defeating contracts. Bonuses and penalties are higher when declarer's side is vulnerable. (page 39)

Waiting Response (of 2♦)—An artificial response of 2♦ to a strong artificial 2♣ opening bid, showing a hand unsuitable for a positive response. (page 96)

Weak Two-bid—An opening bid at the two level in a suit, other than 2♣, typically showing a six-card suit and about 5-11 high-card points. (page 72)

Where—The strain in which the contract should be played: clubs, diamonds, hearts, spades, or notrump. (page 4)

Visit our web site to get
up-to-date information from Better Bridge.

www.BetterBridge.com OR www.AudreyGrant.com

PRODUCTS

Better Bridge material is prepared with the assistance of the Better Bridge Panel of world-wide experts and is available through books, disks, videos, magazines, and the Internet.

BRIDGE TEACHERS

Join the Better Bridge Teachers' Group if you are involved in bridge education. Teacher's manuals are available to assist in presenting bridge lessons to students.

CRUISES

When traveling by ship, add Bridge at Sea and you have a magic fit. Audrey Grant and the Better Bridge Team personally conduct bridge cruises to locations around the world.

FESTIVALS

Workshops and festivals personally conducted by Audrey Grant and the Better Bridge Team are held world-wide. Come with or without a partner...let us get a fourth for bridge.

BRIDGE QUIZ

Try the regularly updated quizzical pursuits. Test your bidding and play, spot the celebrities, and play detective at the table.

BRIDGE ONLINE

Playing bridge on the internet is becoming an increasingly popular pastime since you can play anywhere, anytime. Find out about the Audrey Grant bridge club and lessons.

TO CONTACT AUDREY GRANT

E-mail:	Audrey@AudreyGrant.com
Phone:	1-888-266-4447
Fax:	1-416-322-6601
Write:	Better Bridge
	247 Wanless Avenue
	Toronto, ON M4N 1W5

Visit our site: www.AudreyGrant.com

To order *Audrey Grant's Color-Coded Cards*,
or any other Audrey Grant publications,
contact **Baron Barclay Bridge Supplies**.

Quantity discounts are available.
We will be happy to send a copy of our free
64-page 4-color catalog upon request.

♠ ♥ ♦ ♣

Baron Barclay Bridge Supplies
3600 Chamberlain Lane, Suite 206
Louisville, KY 40241
U.S. and Canada: 1-800-274-2221
Worldwide: 502-426-0410
FAX: 502-426-2044
www.baronbarclay.com

♠ ♥ ♦ ♣

You may send a fax, order online,
or leave an order on our voice mail anytime.